'Grace And Truth' Under Twelve Aspects

William Paton Mackay

Nabu Public Domain Reprints:

You are holding a reproduction of an original work published before 1923 that is in the public domain in the United States of America, and possibly other countries. You may freely copy and distribute this work as no entity (individual or corporate) has a copyright on the body of the work. This book may contain prior copyright references, and library stamps (as most of these works were scanned from library copies). These have been scanned and retained as part of the historical artifact.

This book may have occasional imperfections such as missing or blurred pages, poor pictures, errant marks, etc. that were either part of the original artifact, or were introduced by the scanning process. We believe this work is culturally important, and despite the imperfections, have elected to bring it back into print as part of our continuing commitment to the preservation of printed works worldwide. We appreciate your understanding of the imperfections in the preservation process, and hope you enjoy this valuable book.

'GRACE AND TRUTH'

UNDER TWELVE ASPECTS

BY

W. P. MACKAY, M.A.,

MINISTER OF THE GOSPEL,
HULL.

'Grace and Truth came by JESUS CHRIST.'—*John's Gospel.*

NEW EDITION REVISED.—ONE HUNDRED AND FORTY-FIFTH THOUSAND.

𝕰𝖉𝖎𝖓𝖇𝖚𝖗𝖌𝖍:
JAMES TAYLOR, 31 CASTLE STREET.
LONDON: J. NISBET AND CO.   HAMILTON, ADAMS, AND CO.
S. W. PARTRIDGE AND CO.   CHICAGO: F. H. REVELL.

MDCCCLXXV.

CONTENTS.

		PAGE
'THERE IS NO DIFFERENCE.'	OUR CONDEMNATION,	1
WOULD YOU LIKE TO BE SAVED?	OUR JUSTIFICATION,	21
'YE MUST BE BORN AGAIN.'	OUR REGENERATION,	37
DO YOU FEEL FORGIVEN?	OUR ASSURANCE,	65
WORK OF THE HOLY SPIRIT,	OUR COMFORTER,	79
'HEAVEN OPENED.'	OUR STUDY,	97
TRIUMPH AND CONFLICT.	OUR STATE,	111
'UNDER THE SUN.'	OUR WALK,	142
'NO CONFIDENCE IN THE FLESH.'	OUR SANCTIFICATION,	172
THE DEVIL.	OUR ADVERSARY.	219
'SERVING THE LORD.'	OUR SERVICE,	236
JUDGMENT.	OUR REWARD,	254

INTRODUCTION.

'THE law was given by Moses: grace and truth came by Jesus Christ.' The law showed what man ought to be. Christ showed what man is, and what God is. The law *was given*, but grace and truth *came*. The word translated 'came' is very strong in the original. It might be rendered 'were impersonated' in Him—always kept in due harmony and proportion. Calvary tells out fully what man's true state is, what God's truth is, and what grace means. The law is what man ought to be to God. Grace tells what God is for me. The first word of law is 'Thou,' the first of grace is 'God' so loved. But it is grace through truth. God has investigated everything, nothing has been overlooked. The greatest sin that any man could possibly commit has been committed, namely, the murder of God's Son. At the same time the greatest grace of God has been manifested.

Man by nature likes neither grace nor truth. He is satisfied neither with perfect justice nor perfect goodness. If John the Baptist comes in righteousness he is hated, and men say he is too harsh, and not human, but hath a devil. If Christ comes in love, He is taunted with being a friend of sinners. So when the righteous requirements of God's law are preached, many people are apt to turn and say, 'Oh yes, but that is too strict; you must allow a little margin for our imperfection.' God says, 'make no provision for the flesh.' Alas! it will take far too much, but allow it nothing. When a sanctified walk, separated from the world and all its belongings is insisted on, a certain class are sure to call this legal preaching. And on the other hand when the grace of God is preached, man's wisdom makes it out to be toleration of evil and lawless licence.

Let us suppose that a convict, who has just finished his term of penal servitude, wishes to lead an honest life. He comes to a man who has a large jewellery establishment, and who requires a night-watchman. He is engaged to watch this house through the quiet hours of the night, when he has everything under him, and every opportunity to rob his employer. On the first evening of his watching he meets one of his old companions, who accosts him, 'What are you doing here?'

'I'm night-watchman.'

'Over this jeweller's shop?'

'Yes.'

'Does he know what you are?'

'No, no, be silent; if he knew, I should be dismissed.'

'Suppose I let it out that you are a returned convict.'

'Oh, I pray don't, it would be my last day here, and I wish to be honest.'

'Well, you'll require to give me some money to keep quiet.'

'Very well, but don't let anyone know.' Thus the poor man would be in sad fear and trembling, lest it should come to the ears of his employer what his previous character had been. He would be in terror lest he should meet any of his old friends, and lest his resources should be exhausted in keeping them quiet.

Let us suppose, however, that instead of the employer engaging the man in ignorance of his character, he went to the convict's cell and said, 'Now I know you, what you are, and what you've done, every robbery you've committed, and that you are worse than you believe yourself to be. I am about to give you a chance of becoming honest, I'll trust you as my night-watchman over my valuable goods.' The man is faithful at his post. He meets old companion after old companion, who threaten to inform upon him. He asks, 'What will you tell about me?'

'That you were the ringleader of house-breakers.'

'Yes, but my master knows all that better than you do, he knows me better than I know myself.'

Of course this silences them for ever. This latter is *grace and truth*. The man had been treated in grace, but on the ground that all the truth was out, that his character was known. It is thus that God deals with us. He deals in grace, but He knows what He is doing, and with whom He is working, even the chief of sinners. The whole truth *is out about* us, and God's grace in the face of this saves,

Introduction

gives a new nature, and puts us down before Himself in the highest places of confidence. Man wonders at this. A wicked companion gets converted, his old associates wonder at his boldness in preaching, (like Peter who had denied Christ, accusing his Jerusalem hearers of having denied Him). They think if his audience only knew what they know, they would be suspicious. God knows us better than we know ourselves, and this is our confidence.

Man does not know GRACE. When unadulterated grace, unmixed grace, the grace of God, God's own love to sinners, is preached, man cannot take it in. 'Oh, this is downright Antinomianism.' This is the cry that was raised against Luther when he preached 'full free justification by grace through faith without the deeds of the law.' The cry that was raised against Paul, that he made void the law, that he told the people they might sin that grace might abound. Now, unless our Christianity provokes this opposition, it is not scriptural Christianity. Unless the gospel we preach, when presented to the natural mind, brings out these thoughts, it is another gospel than Paul's. Every Christian, —mark, not some of them—has the Antinomian or God-dishonouring 'flesh' within him to be watched over and mortified; but this is a different matter. People will readily quote 'Faith without works is dead,' 'We must have works,' and so on; and we most certainly coincide. But follow up the argument by inquiry about the works, and you will too often find that such have very loose ideas of Christian holiness. Such will quite go in for having a Christian name, going religiously to church, being able to criticise a sermon and a preacher, being acquainted with good people, abstaining from all immorality, being honest and respectable; but the moment we cross the boundary line that separates respectable and easy-going make-the-most-of Christianity, into the rugged, thorny path of identification with a rejected Christ, separation from the world's gaieties, splendours, and 'evil communications,' dead to it and all that is therein, taking up Christ's yoke, and denying self,—we are met with the expressions, 'too far,' 'pietism,' 'righteous over much,' 'we don't like extremes,' 'legal preaching.'

The *grace of man* would be this, 'Do the best you can by

the help of grace, and then wherein you fail grace will step in and make up.' But the first thing the *grace of God* does is to bring '*salvation*.' (Titus ii. 11.)

Or, again, man's grace may take this shape, 'Oh yes, we believe in the blood, the precious blood of Christ—only faith can save—; and now we have found an easy road to heaven—a sort of short cut in which we can live on good terms with the world and worldly men, and also on first-rate terms with religious men, spend our money to make ourselves comfortable, get a name, honour, or riches here, make ourselves as happy as can be in this world, just take of it what we can enjoy, and go on thus so nicely to heaven.' This is another view of the *grace* that *man* knows about; but the *grace of God* teaches us 'that, denying ungodliness and worldly lusts, we should live soberly, righteously, and godly in this present world, looking for that blessed hope and the glorious appearing of the great God and our Saviour Jesus Christ.' (Titus ii. 12.) Thus man knows nothing whatever about the GRACE of GOD.

Neither does man know TRUTH. He does not know the *truth* about God. He can quite believe that God made the world, and that He is good to a certain extent; but that God looks upon one sin as making a man guilty as really as ten thousand, he cannot understand. Though written as clearly as writing can make it in the Book of God, he cannot perceive it. Christ brought out the truth about God, that He could by no means clear the guilty, but that he could impute guilt and impute righteousness. An infidel said, 'Is it justice for an innocent man to die for a guilty—is it consistent with reason, either in justice to the innocent or the guilty.' 'Well, suppose it is not, and we may grant it. But what if God became man, and put away sin by the sacrifice of Himself—where is your reasoning now? Our gospel is not merely an innocent man dying for the guilty but the God-man being made sin, and putting it away.' Nor does man know the truth about himself, that he is lost. He thinks that he *may be* lost, not that he *is* lost. He hopes, in some vague way, that it will yet be all right with him. Christ brought out the truth about man, that man was hopelessly gone in sin, that he would kill God if he could.

'How few there are in hell who ever intended to be there!' 'Are you to be in heaven?' Most people will answer, 'I hope so.' 'And what right have you to hope so?' I once quietly said to a poor woman who looked as like a good person as any of her neighbours, 'If you have believed in the Lord Jesus Christ, why not say so and thank Him, and then begin to hope (not for pardon, there is no such hope in Scripture) for salvation that is to be revealed at perfected redemption? and if not, what right have you to have such presumption as hoping to get to heaven when you have not believed in the Lord Jesus Christ?' I saw her some time after, radiant with settled joy and peace, and she said, 'Yes, sir, you asked me what right I had to hope, and I was rather astonished; but I did not take your word about it, I went home to my Bible, and there I found that if I was without God, I was without hope in this world.' (Eph. ii. 12.) This led her to discover 'the sand' on which she had been building, and by God's Spirit she was led to 'THE ROCK.'

Look at a perfect illustration of grace and truth in the case of the Gentile woman. (Matt. xv. 21-28.)

'Then Jesus went thence, and departed into the coasts of Tyre and Sidon.' When? After He had exposed the utter hollowness of man's religion, and the character of the Pharisees' heart. In the beginning of the chapter man brought his religion to Christ, and of course Christ showed that it was the heart He dealt with, and not religion.

Verse 8 shows us where the heart of man is—with his religions, his traditions of the elders, his observances, his washing of hands, cups, dishes, tables. It is 'far from God.' Verse 19 shows us what his heart has in it: 'Evil thoughts, murders, adulteries, fornications, thefts, false witness, blasphemies.' This is what happens when man comes to God with his religion—with what he has. 'Do you want to know where you are, and what you are?' Bring your religion to God. But Jesus now goes away to where there is no religion, but plenty of misery; no professions, but a great deal of need. He had shown what man's heart has in it— He now wishes to show what is in His heart—a heart that is 'full of grace and truth.'

'And behold a woman of Canaan came out of the same

coasts, and cried unto Him, saying, 'Have mercy on me, O Lord, thou Son of David; my daughter is grievously vexed with a devil.' She was a Syrophœnician, a Greek, a Gentile, outside the Jewish territory, a dog in the eyes of every godly Jew. 'Without are dogs.' The dog in the East is not as here domesticated, but is more like a wolf prowling for prey outside the cities—fit emblem of those dwellers by the highways and hedges of Luke xiv., the Gentiles outside the Jewish circle of blessing; and thus we are called 'Gentile dogs.' She had no claim on the 'Son of David.' 'He came to His own.' Her need, her desire, her heart, her faith, were in the right direction; but she must intelligently take the right place in order to be blessed. Her instincts were right, her apprehension of the truth was wrong.—This is the reason of that wonderful next word.

'But He answered her not a word.' Many think that this was merely to try her faith—certainly it was to try her faith, but God accomplishes many ends by one means. He has to manifest not only *grace*, but also *truth*. Had He, as 'Son of David,' blessed her, He would not have kept His true place, for 'He was a minister of the circumcision for the truth of God, to confirm the promises made unto the fathers.' (Rom. xv. 8.) And she was 'afar off, an alien from the commonwealth of Israel.' He, as Son of David, 'confirmed the promises;' she was a 'stranger from the covenants of promise;' and when she tried that door, she found it righteously shut, because He is faithful and true. He could have no words with her till He got His own and the only place in which He could rise above all dispensational thoughts, and let His grace flow forth. Claims of truth had to be settled first, then the fountain of grace could flow; but her need kept her at the footstool. She asked ignorantly, but she was in earnest.

And His disciples came and besought Him, saying, 'Send her away; for she crieth after us.' One or other of two courses they might suggest. Peter might have said, 'she is a Gentile dog; she has no right to you as Son of David; send her away.' This would have been *truth*, but at the expense of *grace*; but the Lord Jesus was showing grace as well as truth. John might have said, 'She is a poor, needy woman, just give her what she wants and send her away.'

This would have been grace, but at the expense of truth. Now Jesus was showing truth as well as grace. This is so like man—he cares for little but his own comfort. 'She crieth after us.' 'Us' always must be consulted. How unlike Him who gave 'Himself for us,' when He came as grace and truth. 'What does it matter about dispensational truths, if sinners are saved?' Such is man's talk—and it matters little to the sinner; but what of God's claims and God's truth? 'We do not study this or that truth because it is not essential.' Essential to you or to God? The disciples could not harmonise grace and truth, and therefore they had to sacrifice the one or the other; but both must be seen. Man would either repel from God as an angry Judge, and give no good news to any sinner, or He would undermine the pillars of His throne by giving universal salvation; but 'grace and truth came by Jesus Christ.' He now takes occasion from the appeal of the disciples to let out a little of His mind.

But He answered and said, 'I am not sent but unto the lost sheep of the house of Israel.' As 'Son of David,' He keeps by His peculiar mission. She does not belong to the lost sheep of Israel's house; how, therefore, can He speak to her or grant her the request she presented? He could not deal as 'Son of David' with a Gentile, because she was not of the house of Israel. Was this not truth, some even would think, to harshness? But this is man's idea of harshness. God's truth is never harsh. Grace without truth is sentimentality. Truth without grace is harshness. All this is only (not to 'send her away,' as was the disciples' easy method, but) to lead her to give Him His true place, and then to take her own true place in which grace could flow to her. Why are we not blessed with God's grace? He is waiting to be gracious.' How long will He wait? Till we give Him His true place, and till we take our true place before Him, where He can bless us. When He speaks, she listens, and now takes up her request again.

Then came she and worshipped, saying, 'Lord, help me.' She did not say she was as good as Israel's lost sheep; but she leaves out the title 'Son of David,' and calls Him Lord. 'If He is but sent to Israel's lost sheep I can't call Him Son of David, and be blessed; but He has another and a higher sovereign name, and that is Lord Jehovah, who can help even me. He won't break down the dispensational wall that keeps the poor Gentile dog away from the promises of the Son of David; but He can rise above it in a power that can reach down to help and succour me.' She gives Him now His true place. This is seen in her not using the title 'Son of David,' but only that one word 'Lord,' His true name to her as a Gentile. 'They that know Thy name will put their trust in Thee.' But she had not quite reached her own true place. She needed something more than help; but Jesus, now addressed as Lord alone, can speak to her and reveal a little more. She listens, believes, and always takes up at each step the thought of the fresh revelation, the words that dropped from His lips, for she was in earnest.

But He answered and said, 'It is not meet to take the children's bread, and to cast it to dogs.' Here is *her* name; is she prepared to take it, as well as to give Him His? Well might she have said, 'Me a dog, forsooth! I know many so-called children of Israel who make a greater profession, and I would not be seen with them.' This would have been natural. When man does not feel his need, he compares himself with others. He vindicates, excuses, palliates himself—'Many make more profession than I do; yet I would be ashamed to do what they do.' Very possibly; that is their business; but what of God's claims on you? She felt that her need was deep, and her answer is according to it. She takes the place the Lord gives her, not what she would choose, but what He indicates.

And she said, 'Truth, Lord. Yet the dogs eat the crumbs which fall from their master's table.' This is the place of power. This is the place of blessing.

1st. 'Truth, Lord.' Any name you please—'a sinner,' 'a dog;' but

2d. If I am a dog, it shall be at your table; and there I'll claim the dog's portion. 'Yet the dogs eat the crumbs.'

   We take the guilty sinner's name,
   The guilty sinner's Saviour, claim.

I am a great sinner! 'Truth, Lord;' yet the great sinner claims the great Saviour. I am the chief of sinners! 'Truth,

Introduction

... yet the chief of sinners claims the chief of Saviours. ... ignorant! 'Truth, Lord;' yet Christ is my wisdom. I ... unrighteous! 'Truth, Lord;' yet Christ is my righteousness. I am unholy! 'Truth, Lord;' yet Christ is my sanctification. I am in bondage! 'Truth, Lord;' yet Christ is ... redemption. That 'yet' is the pleading of need from the ... that truth has given.

> Mercy and truth are met together;
> Righteousness and peace have kissed each other.

And now, what is the answer, and what the result? 'Then Jesus answered and said unto her, "O woman, great ... faith; be it unto thee even as thou wilt."' This was ... answer, the very resources of Jehovah thrown open for her ... 'And her daughter was made whole from that hour.' ... was the result, 'From that hour.' What hour? ... hour in which she said, 'Truth, Lord.' The hour in which she took the dog's place, and claimed the dog's portion, ... but a crumb from His blessed table! What must the ... be, when the Church of God, gathered out of Jew ... Gentile, shall sit down at the marriage supper of the ... and every prayer shall have ended, because all shall ... been answered; and the combined glory of grace and ... shall shine out for ever from the brows of all the myriads ... saved by grace, who came in all their degradation ... to the feet of Christ, giving Him His true place, and ... their true place! Friend, God now waits to be gracious ... but you must take the dog's place.

... the following papers I have tried to preserve the ... between GRACE AND TRUTH. 'The grace of God' ... salvation, this is the truth of Titus ii. 'The righteousness' of God;—God being just and justifying Him that ... in Jesus is the truth of Rom. iii. I have endeavoured to show both the grace and truth of God:—

... With regard to the justification of a sinner. Grace ... is seen and truth seen, each equal to the other.

... With regard to the sanctification or growth in grace ... Grace is seen and truth is seen. 'Being made ... from sin, and become servants to God, ye have your fruit unto holiness, and the end everlasting life.' (Rom. vi. 22.)

I here give the thread on which the papers in this volume are crystallized :—

1st. '*There is no difference,*' for until a man sees this, he is not in the place where God can bless him. This is fundamental.

2nd. *Would you like to be saved?* 'Whosoever will' is pointed to the work of Christ for sinners.

3rd. '*Ye must be born again*'—Wherein are discussed the necessity and nature of regeneration. Regeneration is an act done at the same time as justification—not a work as many seem to think, confounding it with gradual sanctification. Justification gives pardon and acceptance. Regeneration gives a new life, a new nature at the same time, perfect in parts but not in development, sanctification being the development of this new life. In this is discussed the question what is the *water*, of which we must be born again.

4th. *Do you feel that your sins are forgiven?* In this is pointed out that most dangerous error of confounding man's feelings with the testimony of God's word—the confounding of the eighth chapter of Romans with the fifth—the confounding of the Spirit's witness to sonship with 'being justified by faith we have peace with God'; that we stand *only* on the written word 'thus saith the Lord' for our 'knowledge of salvation', as we stand only on the incarnate Word for that salvation itself.

5th. *The work of the Holy Spirit.* The connection and difference between the work of the Spirit in me and Christ's work for me are here considered. Many souls would wish to study the work of the Spirit in them first, but only a saved man can profitably study this; one who has come through the former chapter 'do you feel that your sins are forgiven.' The Holy Ghost is never mentioned in Romans till the fifth chapter. Misplaced truth is the worst error.

6th. '*Heaven opened.*' In which we get a glimpse of the counsels of God in the past, present, and future. Heaven is opened now for us and all that is there is ours. The epistle to the Hebrews discloses our opened heaven.

7th. *Triumph and Conflict* come next. The conflict befor

between me and God, now it is between me and myself, and this will be a life-long conflict, for every Christian is in the world, has the flesh within and Satan against him. These are typified by Israel—in Egypt, which is spiritually *the world*—in the Wilderness, where Amalek (the *flesh*) has to be defeated—and in Canaan, where the Canaanites ('*spiritual wickednesses*') have to be overcome. This 'Satanic trinity' is considered in the three following papers in detail.

8th. '*Under the sun.*' Our great foe 'the world' is here looked at. What is it? and how is it to be overcome?

9th. '*No confidence in the flesh*'—the believer's beacon fire. Here we consider what true holiness is and what it is not. Not the old nature made better, but the believer as a whole, as an individual, made better by his new nature keeping the old under. In this is shown the all-important truth concerning the existence in the one individual saved man of two distinct natures. The one person has two natures, one that cannot sin because born of God, the other that cannot but sin because born of Satan. Our practical holiness does not consist in assimilation, but in opposition—not in improvement of the old man, but in his mortification. Our responsibility remains in the *individual* person, possessed of these two natures.

10th. *The devil.* The truth so plainly shown in Scripture concerning the real personal existence, and not mere influence of the devil; where he is, what he is doing, and our power over him, are stated.

11th. '*Serving the Lord*' now comes in. Since we are made free from our foes, since our bands are loosened, we now serve. 'Let my people go that they may serve me.'

12th. *Judgment* is looked at as past with regard to the believer's person, present as to the believer's ways, and to come for the believers works. Many Christians fail to see the perfect balance here between grace and truth— grace putting us for ever beyond judgment, and truth bringing up at the judgment-seat of Christ all our deeds done in the body, good or bad.

In issuing the *hundredth thousand* of this work we have made a few corrections, in order if possible to make our meaning plainer. At the same time we would record our adoring thanks to Him whose name is Wonderful, for having in any way used these pages as the means of sending light into dark hearts, or of solving difficulties for those who already knew His grace and truth, and leading them more intelligently to walk with Himself; and that it has found its way into the hands of tens of thousands of anxious enquirers or earnest Christians in these times of blessing with which our country is now being favoured.

May the gracious Spirit whose work it is to lead into all truth bless what is His own in these pages, to the glory of the ever blessed Lord Jesus Christ, our God and Saviour.

W. P. M.

The Park, Hull,
    1st January, 1875.

"There is no Difference."

OUR CONDEMNATION.

'YOU are always preaching and writing that the vilest and most unworthy are welcome to come to Christ, but what of those that do not feel so very vile?' a sister in the Lord once said to me.

This is a most important question, in regard to a class of people very difficult to reach. She told me that a friend, after having heard a preacher of the gospel describing the awful state of unsaved people, and giving a solemn exhortation to be saved immediately, said, with great surprise, '*But what is it all about? I feel as happy as a bird.*' She really could not understand that the words of the preacher had any reference to her.

Such people never did anything very bad. They have been trained up under all the influences of a christianized society. They never knew vice in its open nakedness. They never felt anything at all very evil in their hearts. They have never been face to face with God, nor taken God's thoughts of sin. In short, they know not the God revealed in Scripture. I do not mean that they are idolaters or infidels in the popular sense of these words. They know a god of their own imagination, a being who is to be heard of in sermons and addressed as a matter of course and religious duty, at times of particular solemnity. They have a few ideas, derived from various sources, of a being called 'God,' but of the God of Holy Scripture they have no knowledge. The God who judges sinners they do not know; God's estimate of sin they have not accepted.

But let me be distinctly understood as to this most important matter. Let us imagine a man wandering on the top of some high cliffs. A bright warm sun is overhead, and a soft green carpet of grass beneath his feet. He feels very happy and gay, but he is going nearer an awful precipice! He is happy, but he is *blind*. We call, we shout to him to stop. He turns round and says, '*What is it all about? I feel as happy as a bird;*' but onward still he goes. Would it not be love on our part to go and take hold of him, and earnestly tell him that a fearful precipice lies a yard before him?

Dear friend, this is where we see you. I have in my mind at this moment an accomplished young lady, amiable, kind, and dutiful, surrounded by all that can make life happy; one who has her neat Bible or Prayer-book, and is seen most regularly and religiously in her seat in church or chapel every Lord's-day, who takes great interest in deeds of charity, visits the poor, and—is very happy. No one ever dared to say to such a one, 'You are on the broad road that leadeth to destruction.' It would be considered highly improper so to do. Perhaps this silent page may be before your eye, and now it would say to you, what has been so long unsaid, 'Stop! are you ready to meet God? where shall you spend eternity?' If you were separated this moment from all the dear friends around you, and all those happy scenes, and that comfortable home, and were standing before God, what would you have to say? I wish to write a little of what He thinks of you. I am not to write about what your parents, your friends, your pastor, or spiritual adviser think of you. They may think most highly of you, and most justly too, as you may be everything that could be desired from a human point of view. But I wish to place before you what God your Maker thinks of you; yes, of you yourself, whoever you may be: the more refined, cultivated, educated, and wealthy you are, the more would I be in earnest to get your attention. You may be a princess or an empress, but one word expresses God's estimate of you, and that word is—'SINNER.'

A rich lady one day, when she heard a person speaking of all as sinners, said with great surprise—

'But ladies are not sinners!'

'Then who are?' she was asked.

'Young men in their foolish days.'

I have not the slightest doubt that this is a very common idea, though seldom expressed.

A lady who had heard some one preaching these truths called on him and said,—

'Do you mean to say that I must be saved just as my footman?'

'Most certainly.'

'Then I shan't be saved.' Poor lady! this was her business, and this was her fatal decision. My reader, I not only wish to tell you that you are a *sinner*—you, educated, amiable lady—but that in God's sight you are just the same as the vilest profligate; just the same before God as that man you heard about who was hanged for murdering his wife. This is most terrible, but it is *true*. I remember once speaking thus to a young man who was not like you, but who knew that he was very bad; and he said,—

'I believe all are sinners, but I don't believe that all are the same.'

'Well, we have only one authority to refer to, and it is within your reach; will you take your Bible, and remember one thing, that it is God who speaks. Turn now to Romans, the 3rd chapter and 22d verse, and at the last clause we read, "For *there is no difference;* for all have sinned, and come short of the glory of God." This is what God has said.'

'Well,' said my friend, 'I never saw that before.'

'But it was there although you never saw it.'

And now, dear reader, you who are happy and amiable, this is the one thing I wish to tell you from God, '*There is no difference.*' This is what you never have felt and never can feel: it is a thing for which you must believe God. As it is God with whom you have to do, I beseech you do not listen one moment to any one who would take you from His truth. *He says* 'there is no difference,' He has proved that the lawless Gentile or heathen and the lawbreaking Jew or religious person are equally guilty, and that not one among either the outwardly profane or the outwardly decent is found righteous or good before Him. Of course there are differences in heinousness or degradation of sins. I need not stop to speak of this; we all know it. I wish to tell you what you and I do not by nature know; namely, that there is no difference as to where we stand before God. The one question is, *guilty* or *not guilty*. There are no degrees as to the fact of guilt. 'He that offends in *one* point is guilty of all,' and nothing less. He that offends in all points, is guilty of all, and nothing more. Therefore, while there are differences among offences, there is no difference as to guilt. Therefore, all men in the world (and you included) have been brought in guilty before God. Look at the story of the Prodigal Son in the 15th of Luke. The moment he crossed his father's threshold with his pockets full of money and a respectable dress on, he was as really guilty, as really a sinner, as when he was among the swine in his rags. He was more degraded when keeping swine, but not more guilty. In fact, his degradation and husks were his greatest mercies, for these led him to see his guilt. A full pocket and a respectable appearance are the worst things a guilty [man] can have, as these lead him to think that he is [rich] and increased with goods, and has need of noth[ing], when in God's sight he is wretched, and misera[ble], and poor, and blind, and naked. I do not [ask] you, Are you a sinner in the common use of th[e] word? because you for whom I write are n[ot.] You mean by sinner, one who is very wild, pro[-] fane, disobedient, and lawless. This is as m[en] speak of sinners. God, however, says that 'th[ere] is no difference.' The only thing I ask you [is] this, Have you offended in one point—not o[ne] point of open sin, but one sin in thought or word[?] You confess to at least one point. God asks n[o] more. If you have offended in one point, *you are guilty of all.* Man would never think this n[or] say it. But God says it. Suppose that your li[fe] were like a book that you had written, and there was only one small blot just like a pin's point in it, whilst all the other leaves were perfectly clean, and you came and presented it before God; He would put it beside all the blackest lives that were ever lived, the blackest histories of the vilest murderers, and thieves, and harlots, and over this collection would be written these words, '*There is no difference.*' For there are but two classes of sinners, the justified and the condemned, and there are only two eternal homes, heaven and hell.

You have offended in one point. It is not a question of being a great sinner—it is this question,

'Are you perfect as the Christ of God, the perfect man?' If you had lived for fifty years without committing one sin, or having one wrong wish or thought, and just then you had an evil thought, and afterwards lived another fifty years and died, aged one hundred, with only this one evil thought (not even a word or an action), when you came to stand before God in judgment, He would put you beside all the offscourings of the earth, men who for a hundred years never had a good thought, and He would say, '*There is no difference.*'

Of course you think this is very hard, but it is true. God will never ask your opinion whether it ought to be so or not. He has in grace told us already what He will do. You and I not knowing absolute holiness, cannot understand or appreciate such a judgment. We could never feel that every one is the same in God's sight as regards guilt. But God says it, and there the matter ends. If you wish to go on, risking your chance of escaping hell on the possibility that God's word is false, and that these words are not perhaps quite true, that '*there is no difference,*' then the judgment-day will declare it to you. I would rather advise you to believe God, against your own ideas and opinions, and simply because He has said it—to proceed as if in His sight '*there is no difference*' between those we call great and little sinners.

'*I cannot believe that all are so bad,*' said one, after I had been saying '*there is no difference.*'

'But,' I added, 'the Bible says, "*there [is no]
difference.*'

'But there must be greater sinners than o[thers].'

'Oh, yes. Most certainly. Great o[ffences]
are recognised in the Bible; he that owed [fifty]
and he that owed five hundred pence; b[ut as to]
guilt, God says, "*there is no difference.*"'

'*Well, I cannot see it,*' still continued [my]
friend.

'*But it is in God's word, whether you see [it or]
not;* and it is sufficient that God has said it[, and]
His Word is truth. Let me give an illust[ration.]
Let us suppose that a bill had been stuck u[p in]
this town, saying that recruits were wante[d for]
Her Majesty's Life Guards, and that none w[ould]
be enlisted but those who were tall, and measu[ring]
not under six feet in height. Let us suppose [that]
many of the young men in the town were anx[ious]
to serve in this regiment. John meets Jam[es,]
and says to him, 'Well, I've more chance th[an]
you, for I am taller than you;' and they [put]
back to back and measure themselves with o[ne]
another, and indeed John is taller than Jam[es.]
And there continues to be much measuring [in]
the town before the day that the recruiti[ng]
sergeant comes.

They measure themselves by themselves, an[d]
compare themselves among themselves, but th[ey]
forget one thing—that not only tall men, bu[t]
men not under six feet are wanted. One man
at last says, 'Well, I've measured myself with
every man in the town, and I'm the tallest man[']

re it," and it might be quite true. But will even he be found qualified?

The trial day comes. Each is measured, from the man five feet six inches, to the very tallest. Suppose he is five feet eleven inches and three-quarters. The sergeant cannot let him pass. He is short. He must take his place among the very shortest as to getting into the Life Guards. He is the tallest man in the town, but he is short of the standard, and 'there is no difference' from the very shortest as to his exclusion from the Life Guards. There is a difference in height, but not in qualification.

Thus it is with every sinner. He may be good, or bad, in the sight of men, but 'there is no difference, for all have sinned and come *short* of the glory of God.' If any man could say, I have come up to God's standard, and this were true, then there would be a difference; but '*come short*' is written on every man's brow, therefore *there is no difference*.

Whether was Adam or Eve the more to blame? This might afford material for a long discussion, and, at the end, the heinousness of their crime would be to us a matter of opinion. I have no doubt there might be some shade of degree as to heinousness; but one thing is sure—if their offences were not equally heinous, they were equally driven out. The cherubim that turned every way with the flaming sword, separated both equally from the tree of life; there was *no difference*.

When the rain began to fall and the water rise, after Noah had entered the ark, those who had their houses high up might have been pitying the poor people who built low down the valley, as they heard the screams of the drowning. By and by the water sweeps over the little hills, and then those on the higher, in turn, congratulate themselves upon their well-built villas. But the water still rises; it enters their ground-floors; they rush out of their grand mansions or hovels—for there was *no difference* —and flee to the tops of the very highest mountains; but only find respite for a few moments, for 'all the high hills, under the whole heaven, were covered; fifteen cubits upward did the waters prevail, and the mountains were covered, and all flesh died that moved upon the earth . . . . . *every* man; *all* in whose nostrils was the breath of life, of *all* that was in the dry land, died, and *every* living substance was destroyed which was upon the face of the ground.' Under that judgment-flood there was *no difference*. Look across the wide level sea, and consider the thousands of caves and stupendous mountain chains that it hides, the plains and valleys, the dens of seaweed and the fortresses of rock; and the level sea rolls equally over all, and there is *no difference*. Drunkard and respectable lady, the hoary-haired sinner and the infant at the mother's breast—all were under that fearful flood, for there was *no difference*. If you had been there, do you think that you would have been made an exception of?

You may be able just now to get anything that money can buy. Could money have saved you then? Prince and beggar, strong men and weak, good and bad, were all equally swept away. There was *no difference*. It has happened already, you see, and it will happen again—not with water, but with fire.

'When Jehovah rained upon Sodom and upon Gomorrah brimstone and fire from Jehovah out of heaven,' there was *no difference*. All were equally destroyed; very bad and very good shared the same fate. This fearful, unprecedented shower falling out of heaven—brimstone and fire—took every one by surprise, and destroyed every dweller there. 'He overthrew those cities and *all* the plain, and *all* the inhabitants of the cities.' There was *no difference*.

When Israel was sheltered in the house of bondage from the destroying angel's hand, 'it came to pass that at midnight Jehovah smote *all* the first-born in the land of Egypt, from the first-born of Pharaoh that sat on his throne, unto the first-born of the captive that was in the dungeon.' Judge and prisoner alike found themselves face to face with death. In the palace and in the hovel the voice of mourning was heard; not one of all the doomed first-born escaped. These first-born might have been beautiful, amiable, educated, and accomplished, or they might have been vile, degraded, ignorant, and hardened; but there was *no difference*. It is with this God that you and I have to do.

'When Jericho's walls fell flat before the appointment, the ordinance of God, in righte[ous judg]ment, the Israelites—'utterly destroye[d all that] was in the city, both man and woman, y[oung and] old.' The strong man and the feeble wo[man, the] active young man and the decrepid o[ld, were] equally slain by the edge of the sword. [There] was *no difference.*

The flaming sword of the cherubim, th[e flood] of waters, the deluge of fire, the angel o[f death,] and Joshua's sword, all preach to you [and me] with calm, decided voice, ' There is *no diff[erence.'*] These things were written for us, that we [may] know what we may expect, so that we migh[t not] leap in the dark. Nothing will happen [that] has not been told us.

A brother in the Lord could never get a y[oung] lady to think about eternity until he quoted [the] text, ' The wicked shall be turned into hell, [and] all the nations that *forget* God.' That wo[rd] '*forget*' seemed to haunt her. May it ha[unt] you, unsaved reader! You do not require to de[ny] God's existence, to mock at Him, to despise Hi[m,] to reject Him, to neglect Him; all you have [to] do is to *forget* God. Do you know the God w[ho] says, '*There is no difference?*' Have you f[or]gotten that he identifies you with all descend[ed] from Adam? Have you forgotten the God w[ho] banished our parents from Eden, and placed [a] sword that cried for blood? Our brother Ca[in] soon forgot, our brother Abel remembered. Ha[ve] you forgotten the God who swept away all i[n] the days of Noah?

Have you forgotten that He is the Judge of quick and dead, and as there was *no difference*, so there is a day coming when there will be *no difference?* In the judgment of the quick, *all the goats* are equally on the left hand—'*there is no difference.*' In the judgment of the dead, 'the dead, *small* and *great*, stand before God'—*small* and *great* sinners, young and old, king and serf, peer and peasant—'and *whosoever* was not found written in the book of life, was cast into the lake of fire,' for '*there is no difference.*' Your name may have been written on the communion-roll of any or all the churches, or it may have been written in the sheets of the Newgate conviction-book for murderers, but 'there is *no difference.*' The lake of fire levels all distinctions. There may be, there are, many and few stripes; there may be, there are, great and small cups full of wrath, but every cup, be it great or small, is *full.* The lake of fire—fearful thought—rolls its hideous sea of wrath and torment in one surging wave over all whose names are not then found in the book of life. In hell, and perhaps only there, for the first time, you will believe that '*there is no difference.*' Every one believes it there.

Let me ask you to look at another picture. Three men are hung on three crosses. If you look at them with the mere eye of sense, you will see that '*there is no difference.*' If you listen to what they are saying, you will hear the one on this side mocking Him in the centre; and the one on the other side saying, 'Dost not thou fear God, seeing thou art in the same condemnation, and we indeed *justly*, but this man hath done nothing amiss.' The one in the centre is saying, 'Father, forgive them, for they know not what they do.' Those suffering 'justly,' and he that did 'nothing amiss,' suffer together, for since He has in His grace taken the sin of the sinner upon Him, He now bears its doom, and 'there is *no difference*.' Those needing forgiveness, and He praying for their forgiveness, are under the same doom, for 'there is *no difference*.' Who are they? Those on either hand are two malefactors, or thieves, who die by the condemnation of their law. He in the centre was proved innocent, and He is the Judge of quick and dead. He has taken of His own free-will the load of sin upon Him, and, under sin, He cannot be cleared. Spotless, pure, holy though He be, He cannot escape. God can by no means clear the guilty. 'He hath made Him sin for us, who knew no sin.' He is under the guilt, and 'there is *no difference*' to the human eye between Him and the thief—He must suffer. Does not this explain all difficulty about an innocent, amiable, virtuous, accomplished lady being on the same level before God as a drunkard and a murderer? Here is God's perfect Son—yea, the very God-man—on the same level with malefactors, not for Himself but for us. God became man, and gave Himself for our sins. This satisfaction that the innocent made for the guilty is offered to you, and you may freely have it, for 'there is *no difference*.'

If the eye of the vilest sinner in this world should perchance rest on this—an outcast from all society, one who has lost all friends and all self-respect, the tottering drunkard coming out of his delirium tremens—I tell you as from God, this Christ is offered to you as God's love-gift. You may reckon Him yours, and proceed upon it as if He were yours, as truly as I or any other person in this world may do so. You have as much right to claim Him as we have, for '*there is no difference*' in God's sight—

> 'His blood can make the foulest clean,
> His blood avails for me.'

Thus, my friend, for whom especially I write this, you have to take the lost sinner's place; for God says, '*there is no difference.*' As I have said before, I could know this only from God's Word. You have been as happy as a bird all your life, but you have forgotten to find out what God thinks about you. I have tried to show you this from the Bible. I do not ask you if you feel it, for I am sure you never could, neither could any one feel all the catalogue of sins in Romans ii. and iii. to be true against him individually; but God knows us better than we know ourselves, and this is His estimate of us.

From the same word, and therefore on the same authority, and on none other, I tell you that God has provided a sacrifice for you—Christ. "For God so loved the world that He gave His only-begotten Son." I do not say that you are to feel

that Christ is yours, any more than I a[sk you to]
feel all the indictment true against you. [Just]
to accept Christ as yours, as you accept t[he]
accusation against you as yours, only, [on the]
authority of God.

I once asked a woman, 'Do you feel [that you]
are condemned?'

'Yes,' she said.

'Now,' I answered, 'that is absurd. Yo[u]
know and *feel* you are guilty, but you ca[nnot]
believe you are condemned, because you kn[ow you]
are condemned on the authority of the jud[ge who]
has pronounced the sentence.'

So on God's authority, and on it alone, I [know]
that I am 'condemned already.' And on th[at]
authority alone I know that 'Christ is for
me individually. Just because I accept G[od's]
estimate of myself, I have a right to accept G[od's]
estimate of His Son for me. I believe the r[ecord]
that God gave of His Son to lost sinners. It [is not]
very humble to say I am too great a sinne[r, or]
something similar, thus comparing myself [with]
other sinners; but the *humbling* bit is that '[there]
is no difference.'

All are 'condemned already,' but only th[ose]
who believe it reap the advantage of this. [Ad]
vantage! What advantage can there be in kn[ow]
ing I am condemned already? Much, beca[use]
only they who believe themselves condemned [will]
claim a Saviour. And now the 'righteousne[ss of]
God is by faith of Jesus Christ unto *all*,' tha[t is]
to say, it is offered, in the person of Ch[rist]

equally to every person in this world, but is only 'upon *all them that believe*; for there is no difference, for all have sinned.' 'All,' in Rom. iii. 9, are said to be '*under* sin.' So in ver 22, all believing ones are under righteousness. It is '*upon* all them that believe.' Righteousness is altogether and for ever outside every man's attainment, for it must be perfect, and all have sinned. Read Rom. iii. 19 to 26. 'Where sin abounded grace did much more abound.' God has proved us all equally by nature and practice '*under sin*;' He now has placed all of us who believe '*under* grace.'

Thanks be unto God, my dear friend, though you began this paper not knowing yourself as God knows you, you may now, on God's authority, where you are, without moving, claim Christ 'the righteousness of God' as yours, and may rise to tell others like yourself what God thinks of us and what God has provided for us. It is in love that He will not let you alone. If we are to be 'before Him' for ever, we must be 'holy and without blame in love;' and if so, it is only 'in His Son' that this can be.

Virtuous or vile, decent or indecent, rich or poor, receive and rest upon God's Christ *now* as He is so freely offered you, and then you may believe (not feel) that your sins are in the depths of the sea, that the shoreless ocean of the love of God flowing through a crucified Saviour has rolled over your millions of sins, and you can triumphantly say, as you look at that ocean covering all that is against you, 'there is [no differ]ence.'

If any one is to be kept out of heaven [for a] believer's sins, it must be Christ, for '[He bore] our sins.' God laid on Him our iniquiti[es.]

Clad in the skins of God's own makin[g (type] of the righteousness of God), Adam and E[ve, being] equally clothed, there was *no difference*.

Shut in by God's hand into the ark of [gopher] wood, 'Noah only remained alive, and th[ey that] were with him in the ark,' but they all, gre[at and] small, man and beast, bird and creeping [thing,] lion and worm, were equally saved, floating [up] and nearer heaven the higher the judgment w[aters] rolled, for there was *no difference*.

Under shelter of the sprinkled blood [every] house of Israel was safe even in Egypt, a[nd all] equally rejoiced around the roasted lamb, [for] there was *no difference*.

Under protection of the scarlet line all f[ound] in Rahab's house were equally safe, when [all in] Jericho were destroyed, for there was *no d[iffer]ence*.

None of all those enrolled in the Lamb's [book] of life can be cast into the lake of fire. T[hey] shall never see the second death, for in that b[ook] there is *no difference*; once there, we are perf[ectly] safe for ever. God's salvation to lost sinners m[ust] always be through judgment. We must a[ccept] His ordinance. What was there in skins of be[asts,] an ark of gopher wood, a few drops of bloo[d, a] red cord, or a certain book? They are G[od's] ordinance, God's perfect way. It will matter little what we think will condemn or save, let us accept God's thoughts for both. God has written out our character. Read Rom. i. 29, 'Being filled with all unrighteousness, fornication, wickedness, covetousness, maliciousness; full of envy, murder, debate, deceit, malignity. Whisperers, backbiters, haters of God, despiteful, proud boasters, inventors of evil things, disobedient to parents, without understanding, covenant-breakers, without natural affection, implacable, unmerciful.' Gal. v. 19. 'Adultery, fornication, uncleanness, lasciviousness, idolatry, witchcraft, hatred, variance, emulations, wrath, strife, seditions, heresies, envyings, murders, drunkenness, revellings, and such like.'

But I hear some one say,

'That is the character of a heathen.'

'Yes, friend, but it is thine also—these are what thy heart is made of. They may be kept under, but they are all there in germ, though not necessarily developed into transgression.'

'Nay, all these are not in my heart.'

'Well, I'm sorry to hear it.'

'Why?'

'Because only this character will be received at Calvary. Only what God has written about us will be accepted by Him; and coming to Calvary with this in our hands, we shall hear His voice saying, "I, even I am He that blotteth out thy transgressions for mine own sake, and will not remember thy sins," and all are gone for ever.'

Why does not every one believe that his heart is desperately wicked? Because it is deceitful above all things, and cannot bear to hear the truth when spoken about itself.

Accept the character God has given you, and accept the Saviour He has provided for you.

> Thou just and holy God
>   Before Thee who can stand?
> Guilty, condemned, all waiting wrath
>   In judgment from Thy hand.
>
> One sin deserves a hell,
>   A death that ne'er shall die;
> Our sins like sands on ocean's shores
>   In millions 'gainst us lie.
>
> Thou God of truth and grace,
>   We praise Thee for Thy way
> By which the guilty may draw near—
>   Their guilt all put away.
>
> Thy Christ who bled and died,
>   Up to Thy Throne has gone;
> Himself Thy love-gift we accept,
>   We rest on Him alone.
>
> We praise Thee as Thy sons
>   Before our Father's face,
> As o'er our every sin now rolls
>   The ocean of Thy grace.

Would You like to be Saved?

OUR JUSTIFICATION.

'WOULD you like to be saved?'
'Indeed I would.'
'And would you like to be saved in God's way?'

'Oh! yes. But I can scarcely see how any poor sinner like me can *know* that I am saved as long as I am in this world.'

'Well, I wish to place before you a sure road to heaven for the unholiest of us all, and shew you how, by simply believing God, we may know that we are saved.'

'I read my Bible, and I am sure I believe every word in it.'

'I know there are few in our land who doubt that there is a God, or disbelieve the leading doctrines of the Bible. But, by the help of the Spirit of God, I would try to tell you some plain truths which you may not know, or about which you may have wrong notions—truths about God's relation to you, yourself, personally and individually, and about your seeing, receiving, and taking for yourself God's salvation.'

'Do you know that GOD loves YOU?'
'Ah! yes,' you say, 'He loves us all.'

'Quite true.' But sit down and ask again, 'Do I believe that God loves me,' convince you of it, He says in His Bible, word is enough from Him—'God so loved world,' and you are part of that world.

But now you say, 'If God so loves me, He be merciful to me a poor, struggling, failing ner, if I do the best I can, and He will over my many sins.' Now, this is a point upon you need to be set right. His name is LOVE He is as just as He is merciful, as true as gracious, and thus 'can by no means clear guilty.' He can overlook nothing. You that the Lord Jesus Christ, God Himself manifest in the flesh, came into our position, our place under our sin, and died a great many years He had no sin of His own, but put away sin the sacrifice of Himself. Now, God says that *so* loved us that He gave us His Son, and all we have to do is to believe in Him. Of course you believe that He came and died; but did ever believe that God gave *Him to you?* 'Ah you say, 'I wish I could *feel* that.' But God does not ask you to feel it. He states what he given to you, and asks you to believe Him. 'God so loved the world that He gave His only begotten Son,' whether you believe it or not. When you accept God's gift you believe in Him.

The Lord Jesus Himself told us this when on earth; and surely He did not mean to deceive us. He was speaking about the bitten Israelites in the wilderness. They were all bitten, and a serpent of brass was put upon a pole, and every one that looked lived. This serpent was given to the Israelites whether they looked or not. Supposing that one Israelite had said, I wish I could *feel* that the serpent is for me, what would you have said? 'Certainly: are you bitten?' That is all you need. 'Are you a guilty sinner?' Then you have a right to accept Christ just as you are. This is the simplicity of the gospel, which has stumbled many great men, and which seems so foolish to the wise of this world.

People, when they are ill, or begin to think they are dying, try to pray, leave off bad habits, and be good, and do the best they can. Yet, though all these are very proper things to do, they will never save anybody. Supposing these bitten Israelites, instead of looking, had begun to put on poultices, and get ointments, and dressings, and mixtures, to counteract the bites—well, that would have been very sensible, men would say; but God said, LOOK; do as I tell you:—LOOK to that serpent on the pole. So God's gospel is, 'Believe on the Lord Jesus Christ and thou shalt be saved.'

But you may say, 'I am no worse than my neighbours. If I am lost many will run a bad chance; there are many worse than I am, and I only hope in God's mercy.' Now, this is all a delusion. One sin will damn any man for ever. Sin brought God's Son from heaven to become man and die. It is true many are worse than you, and that they will have a bad chance. That is the very reason I write this for you, and because most people are living without [Christ?] now and do not know it. I did not [make any] calculation. The Lord Jesus Christ, who [cannot] lie, said that there were two roads, [a wide] and a narrow, that most people go in the [wide] one, and few go in the narrow one, [that the] wide one ends in endless misery, and the narrow one in endless happiness. You have only [one] chance, which is to believe God who says [that] one sin will send you to hell. 'Whosoever [shall] keep the whole law, and yet offend in one [point], he is guilty of all' (Jas. ii. 10). You have committed at least one sin. Now accept Christ [as] your own and only Saviour.

But the great deceiver of the world, that is the devil, who tries to do all he can against God's truth, if he finds that you will not believe yourself to be worse than other people, or that still [you] have a chance, will take another and an opposite course, for the devil's statements are like the time of a bad watch, either too fast or too slow. He tells you that either you are too bad or not [bad] enough. Now, the Lord Jesus Christ came [to] seek and to save the lost. A man who said [of] himself that he was the chief of sinners is in heaven long ago. The blackest, vilest, most debased, most debauched, polluted, filthy, unclean, hard-hearted, evil-tempered, lying, covetous, thieving, murderous, grey-haired sinner that ever tottered on this side of the grave, is reached by Him who hung between two thieves for sin. God says it: that is all. We cannot understand it. Only this, He chose to do it, and now He tells us. A thief that had reviled Christ after the hand of death was on him is in Paradise, we know. Why not you? And why not be saved now? If not now it may be never.

I once met a poor woman in the south of England. I began to speak to her about heaven and Christ. She did not understand me. I asked her if she had ever heard of the Lord Jesus; she said, NO (most lamentable in this Christian land, so called). I told her that up above those skies the Lord Jesus dwelt, and He had so loved us that He had descended from heaven and become a man. There was a condemned criminal lying waiting execution not far from where we were, and every one was speaking about him. I said to her, 'You have heard about the man that is to be hanged.'

'Ah yes.'

'Suppose, as he lay in the jail the night before the execution, a knock were heard at the door, and a gentleman walked in, sat down, and said,—

' "You have broken the laws."

' "Yes, yes," the convict would cry.

' "You have been condemned."

' "Yes, yes, justly too."

' "You are to be hanged."

' "Yes, to-morrow."

' "I am the Queen's son; I have come from Windsor at her Majesty's desire, and this is what

that He so loved YOU (put in *your* [name]
He gave His Son for YOU (put in yo[ur name];
that is faith). As I have said, but wo[uld say]
again, you have not to *feel* that Christ [died,]
but to *believe* God that He is. If you [be-]
lieve Him, all your sin is for ever go[ne, be-]
tween you and God you are justified [from all]
things, your sins are cast into the depths of [the sea,]
you can never come into condemnation, [you are]
as sure of heaven as if you were there, for [His]
Word is pledged to it. Certainly your [evil]
heart within you is not gone. I have of[ten met]
with poor distressed souls who were una[ble to]
make out how people could know they were [saved,]
thinking that if they were saved they [would]
never have any sin in them. God says, if [we]
(that is *saved* people) say they have no sin [we]
deceive themselves. All the difference lies in [my]
having sin IN me, and sin ON me. I once t[ried]
to put the way to be saved before a little girl [who]
was wishing to know about it, and I think [God]
shewed her the gospel to the saving of her soul.

'How many people were crucified on Calva[ry?']

'Three,' she replied. 'Two thieves, and Je[sus]
between.'

'Were both the thieves equally bad?'

'Yes, they suffered justly.'

'Did both die alike?'

'No.'

'What made the difference?'

'One believed on Jesus, the other did not.'

'Now what about sin with regard to the[se]

three? The one thief that did not look to Christ, had he sin IN him?'

'Yes.'

'Had he sin ON him?'

'Yes.'

'And Christ, had He sin IN Him?'

She thought a little, but she answered rightly, 'No.' (He was holy, harmless, no speck ever defiled Him, He could touch lepers and still be clean).

'Had He sin ON Him?'

'Yes.'

'His own?'

'No.'

'The thief that looked to Christ, had he sin IN him after he looked?'

'Yes.'

'Had he sin ON him?'

'No.'

This Cross still divides the world. We are all sinners, as were both the thieves. On one side are saved sinners, on the other unsaved sinners. On the one side are those who believe God that Christ is for them; on the other, those who do not. On the one side are those who have sin IN them, but no sin ON them, because they have left it on the spotless Sin-bearer; on the other, those who have sin both IN them and ON them. And all the people in the world die as those two thieves did. None ever died, or ever will die, without sin IN them. The name of every man when he dies will be *sinner*. The name of each

man was *thief* to the very last bre[ath]
died a saved *thief*, the other died an un[saved]

The one set of men die saved sinner[s,]
unsaved sinners. The one die with sin
sinking them down to an awful hell;
die with no sin on them, and are 'for e[ver with]
the Lord.'

'Now, will you not be saved?'

'How *can* I?'

'Simply LOOK.'

'But I have often tried to look, and
often tried to bring before my mind a pic[ture of]
Jesus hanging on the cross for me.'

'Now, that is not the way at all: a vi[sion of]
Christ on the cross, or a dream, or a thou[ght, is]
not what God gives. Suppose I was laid o[n my]
death-bed to-night, and, as I lay, the devil [came]
to me, and told me that I was not saved; su[ppose]
I said to him, "Some time ago I had a visi[on of]
Christ hanging on the cross for me."

'"Ah!" he would say, "that was a delusi[on]
brought before your eyes to deceive you."

'"Well, but I dreamt one night that Christ c[ame]
close to me, and said, 'Thou art mine.'"

'"It was all a delusion."

'"I had a thought one day: it just flashed acr[oss]
me all at once, that I was saved."

'"Only a delusion." And I could not ans[wer]
the accusing deceiver. But I will tell you wh[at]
will put him to flight. I take my Bible and
say, "God *says* that He gave me Christ."

'"How do you know that Christ is for you

' "Because God SAYS that He so loved the *world* that He gave His only begotten Son."

' "But do you think that so great a sinner as you can be saved by simply accepting Christ as God's gift?"

' "Yes; for God *says*, 'He that believeth on the Son HATH everlasting life.'" And the devil could say nothing; for it is written, "They overcame him by the blood of the Lamb and by the *word* of their testimony." You see I would never dare to bring before him what I felt or what ideas had crossed my mind, but simply and solely *what* God *says*. This is *looking to*—this is seeing Christ in the *Word of God.*'

'Will you not be WASHED in His *blood*, and be made for ever clean?'

'But how can I? What do you mean by His blood? I have often heard about it, and have often tried, while lying on my bed, to bring before my eyes the sight of His blood flowing from His wounded hands and feet, and from His pierced side.'

'Now this is another mistake: blood is a figure for *life taken*. Seeing the blood means believing God about the death of His Son, instead of your death. Being satisfied with Christ's death in the room of yours, this is being washed in the blood. You see no real blood, nor vision, nor picture of blood; but in that blessed Book of God you read, "He was wounded for our (faith says *my*) transgressions, He was bruised for our iniquities, the chastisement of our peace was upon Him, and

with His stripes we are healed." [...]
is seeing the blood.'

'Will you not COME to Christ?'

'But how can I? I have read in [...]
that He said, "Come unto Me, all ye th[...]
and are heavy laden, and I will give y[...]
and I have often wished I had been [...]
when He was here—wished I had seen [...]
my door; I would have watched Him, [...]
run to Him and touched his garment. [...]
is in heaven and how can I come to Him?'

'Now God has most beautifully explain[ed...]
for we have not to go up to heaven (Rom[...]
to bring Him down, nor to go to the g[...]
bring Him up; but He is risen and gone to h[...]
and He has left His WORD, in which alon[e...]
can now be found. This Word may be in [...]
hands and in your memory, that Word whic[h...]
Holy Ghost has written, and is now urging [...]
to believe, that God so loved you as to give [...]
Son for you. He is asking you in that Wor[d...]
accept His gift. This is 'coming to Christ.' [...]
that He is in heaven, His Spirit and His W[ord...]
—His Word from His lips, and His Spirit [...]
through, and with the Word, are all that are le[ft...]
and will these not satisfy? Have you nev[er...]
thought that if you saw your name written in t[he...]
heavens, or on the sea-shore, and you knew th[at...]
it had been traced by God's finger, you woul[d...]
then believe that you were saved; but do yo[u...]
think God will make another and special revel[a-]
tion for you? No, no—you must just take [...]

vation as all the rest of us poor sinners have taken it, by believing the one Book.'

'But have I not to wait God's time?'

'God has only one time—that is, to-day. I read of to-morrow in the Bible. Pharaoh wished the frogs taken from him, but—to-morrow. To-morrow is man's time. Now, to-day, is God's. If you came to a stream, would you sit down and say, I will wait till it flows past and when it is dry, then I will cross? Men are not such fools. God is waiting on you. He is calling you. He is beseeching you; and this is His one request, Take my Son whom I have given. He cries to every accountable and rational soul in this world, Will you have Him?'

'Oh, if I could feel a something in me telling me that Christ was mine, I would believe it.'

'Quite wrong again. It is believing something outside you, trusting Him at God's right hand, and resting on His *sure, eternal Word.*'

'But must I not repent?'

'Most certainly; but this beautiful, comprehensive, and scriptural word has been so abused that it is almost dangerous to use it to an anxious soul. Most unsaved people think that by repentance is meant bringing to God a certain amount of sorrow for sin, quite undefined as to quantity or quality, for which God will justify them. This is the worst phase of legalism. The word "repentance" covers much. Its first step is when the sinner obtains

'"A true sense of his sin." Th[us he]
accepts God's estimate of his sin ra[ther than his]
own estimate. He takes the lost [sinner's place and]
accepts the character that God has [given him.]
The next step is

"The apprehension of the mercy [of God in]
Christ." He accepts the provision th[at God has]
made, and now, being a saved man he [is a godly]
man, and thus can have godly sorrow. [The]
sorrow that a man has before he appreh[ends the]
mercy of God in Christ is mere sorro[w at the]
prospect of being punished for sin. Godl[y sorrow]
is on account of the sinfulness of sin. Th[us,]
after a man apprehends the mercy of [God in]
Christ, he then "doth with grief and ha[tred of]
his sin turn from it unto God, with full p[urpose]
of and endeavour after new obedience." [This is]
scriptural repentance, which has become [dis-]
torted by reasoning man.'

You will not throw this aside, will you[? Do not]
say, I like it, or I do not like it? The poo[r sin-]
ner, saved by the grace of God, who writes t[o you]
cannot save you, nor can any man. Tell [God]
what you are to do; tell God that He loves [you;]
tell God that you trust Him; tell God that [you]
believe Him; tell God that He has given you [His]
Son; tell God that you believe *that* also; [tell]
God that He laid all your sins upon Christ; [tell]
God that you believe they were *on Him*, [and]
therefore are not *on* you; tell God you have g[one]
astray, but that you believe Him that your i[ni-]
quity was laid on Christ. Thank God for

finished salvation in Christ. Tell Him how well pleased He is with the Lord Jesus instead of you tell Him that you are

'A poor sinner and nothing at all,
But Christ the Lord is your all in all.'

May God Himself shew you, for His name's sake, His simple Gospel of *Christ for you.* A beloved brother said, when coming out of the darkness of self, 'It is the simplicity that stumbles me. It is too good news to be true.' Yes, if man were in it; but it is not too good when we consider with what a God we have to do. You see God can overlook nothing. He can FORGIVE anything. He can by no means clear the guilty. He can take us out of the guilty Adam-standing, and put us into a new, a resurrection Christ-standing. He can save to the uttermost the blackest, vilest sinner that accepts (simply accepts) His gift, Christ. Will you not receive Him? You may be in poverty, in nakedness, in misery, but God presents you with His Son. He might have created a world for every one of us; but that would have been nothing compared with what He has given—the LORD JESUS CHRIST. You may have great difficulty here to make ends meet, but having Christ it will be all the hell you will ever be in. You may have every comfort, and be altogether moral and good as far as man can judge, upright and religious, but without Christ this will be all the heaven you will ever have. Religiousness, goodness, kindness, benefi-

cence, uprightness, amiability, will n...
Acceptance of God's gift alone will do...

Now, what is it to be, ere we p...
never to converse again for ever—G...
gospel for the meanest, poorest, weak...
so that even a fool may embrace it;...
ways, follies, pleasures, religion, world...
is offered to all. Some will accept...
some will refuse. You make God a li...
refuse Him. You make yourself a liar,...
true, if you accept Him. Some may k...
about Christ the gift of God presented...
and yet not know Himself. ' 'Tis eternal...
know Him.' By not receiving Him, they t...
under foot the blood of the life-giving...
Others receive Him and thank God for H...
are saved.

May the blessed Spirit, the witnesser of...
open the eyes of every reader to see Him,...
every fellow-sinner to believe God, and...
His gift.

Call your heart a liar, and believe the...
of the only living and true God.

> There is nothing to do, for being born 'dead,'
> You must have another to work in your stead;
> Christ Jesus, in Calvary's terrible hour,
> Has done all the work in such marvellous power,
> That, raised from the dead, He now offers to you
> Life, pardon, salvation, and nothing to do!
> No, nothing to do till you're saved from your sins,
> When the power of doing good only begins.

'Ye Must be Born Again.'

OUR REGENERATION.

THOUGH you knew all the duties incumbent upon a royal prince, this knowledge would not make you a royal prince. You must be in a position before you can act under the laws of that position. This is the natural order admitted by all men in human things, but quite reversed when they begin to speculate on divine things. God's order is this—I make you sons: walk like sons. Man says, Try to walk like sons, and after a shorter or longer time you will be made sons. But we must be brought out of the kingdom of darkness before we can take the first step in the kingdom of light. Before we can enter this kingdom we must have a nature capable of enjoying it. A nature can be implanted only by birth; therefore we must be born again. This subject is gone fully into in John iii.

Nicodemus, a ruler of the Jews, came to Jesus, and said to Him, 'WE KNOW,' &c.

Our Lord answered him by saying, 'EXCEPT A MAN BE BORN AGAIN,' &c.

There is a great difference between what we *know* and what we *are;* a great difference between our attainments, education, talents, knowledge

and our standing before God, and [...]
God. Nicodemus was an inquir[...]
had been convinced of Christ's claim[...]
evidences, and whose conscience was [...]
after something deeper and more sati[...]
what he possessed. He comes with this [...]
of knowledge—'Rabbi, we know that [...]
teacher come from God: for no man c[an do the]
miracles that thou doest, except God [be with]
him.' (John iii. 2.) The Lord Jesus, [who]
knew all men, and all the thoughts of [men, an-]
swered not the words but the need of Nic[odemus]
by shewing that all his knowledge woul[d not]
save him or any other man; for 'Except [a man]
be born again, he cannot see the kingdom [of God.']
Nicodemus by nature, however well-inst[ructed,]
could never see God's kingdom.

I.—CHRIST NOT A TEACHER OF THE OLD NAT[URE.]
HE IS FIRST A SAVIOUR, THEN A TEACHER.

In the present day, in certain quarters, we [hear]
a good deal about Christ as the perfect m[an, the]
perfect example, and the perfect teacher; but [what]
is the answer of the Lord Himself to all [these]
compliments. He came not to teach the [old]
nature—not to teach man as sprung from A[dam,]
but to seek and save the lost, to give th[em a new]
nature, and to teach saved men. The p[olicy]
of all who have openly, or in thought, denie[d the]
divinity of Christ, is to laud His moral teach[ing]
and his God-like example. They bring w[ell-]
known and fondly-cherished truths forward, a[nd]

only they believed and preached these great facts; but at the outset they forget this insurmountable barrier to all moral reclamation of the old nature of man, 'Except a man be *born again*, he cannot see the kingdom of God.'

We find others, however, who not merely know Christ as a teacher, but who also believe in His divinity, that He is God as well as man. In fact, many in our land know every fundamental doctrine in the Bible; but a mere knowledge of doctrine, however true, never introduced a son of Adam into the kingdom of God. Men may have learned what justification and sanctification and adoption are; they may be able to distinguish minutely between all the creeds, 'isms,' and heresies; they may be theoretically orthodox, may be able to judge preachers and sermons, may be very ready freely to criticise most men they hear, and graciously to pay beautiful compliments to their special favourites, as Nicodemus did to our Lord; they may know, moreover, about the new birth, its necessity and divine origin; but notwithstanding all this, they could not dare to say, as before God, 'Whereas we were blind, now we see.' The greatest amount of theological education never yet saved a man. Creed, or the belief in a certain amount of doctrine, has made Christendom, but never made a Christian—'Ye must be born again.'

Others again, when their consciences have been reached, try to get this new birth brought about, and begin most zealously to train and trim, to educate and reform their old nature, [...] of what is meant by '*born again*.'

II.—THE OLD NATURE UNCHANGED [AND] UNCHANGEABLE.

Nicodemus wondered how a man, [who] could be brought again into this world; [if it] were possible, what better would he be? [He] might have changed his circumstances [by a] new birth according to the flesh; but w[ould he] have changed kingdoms? He would st[ill be in] the kingdom of the first Adam; he would [be] flesh; for our Lord goes on to say, 'Tha[t which] is born of the flesh is flesh' (ver. 6). [It] never rose above its level: that which is pro[duced] is of the same nature as that which produ[ces.] We find people to-day who think that if [they] were in other circumstances they would h[ave a] better chance of getting saved. The rich [man] thinks that if he were poor, he might have [time] to think of religion. The poor man, if he c[ould] get ends to meet, and had a little more mo[ney,] would have more leisure to think of God. [But] the difficulty is not so much in what is *aroun[d]* as in what is *within* us.

Again, the aids of religion are called in, [in] order that *the flesh* may be *improved*; but a[fter] all attempts, it is found to be only religious fle[sh.] Man may have all varieties of it; but it ne[ver] rose to see the kingdom of God. In nature, [we] speak of the animal kingdom and the vegeta[ble] kingdom. If we took a rose from the latter these kingdoms, and cultivated it and trained it, and by our various arts made it produce all its varieties, we never by these means could bring it into the other kingdom—into the animal kingdom. Or again, if I take a nettle from the roadside, and bring it into my garden or my hothouse, watch over, dress, water, and warm it, I may produce beautiful nettles, and beautiful varieties of nettles, but I never could get apples from it; that which is produced from the nettle is nettle. We can never gather grapes from thorns, nor figs from thistles.

Man by nature is in the kingdom of the first Adam: no amount of reformation, amelioration, cultivation, civilisation, or religiousness, can bring one single man into the kingdom of God. Look through Great Britain and Ireland—what is the object of the great bulk of the religious machinery in existence? Is it not to cultivate the flesh, in order that, after death, it may see the kingdom of God? This is no guess. It is the sad confession of godly men in all the churches—godly bishops, godly rectors, godly pastors, elders and deacons. All unite in the same complaint, and do their best against it. The majority of respectable religious people, as good as Nicodemus, a master in Israel, do not know the practical power of this truth which stands at the door of God's kingdom. They put salvation at the end of a long series of self-improving processes. God puts the salvation of the soul at the very beginning, and all duties that in their discharge can honour Him, are founded upon this fact. 'Man's chief end is' (not to get the soul saved, but) 'to glorify God and to enjoy Him for ever'—starting with being saved for nothing as the means to this end.

III.—THE ABSOLUTE NECESSITY OF A NEW NATURE.

Before I can enter God's kingdom I must have a new nature that can appreciate, see, live in, and enjoy that kingdom. Ask a blind man what red is. He has no idea of it because he cannot see, because he has not the capacity. Educate him in the mixing of colours. Tell him that blue and yellow mixed make green; he may soon remember this, and *know* much more; by that knowledge he can never see a colour.

The questions therefore of most importance to you are not, do you know doctrine? do you know Christ's teaching? do you know your Bible? do you know the evidences of Christianity? do you know that Christ is God, that Christ is a Saviour? that He is able and willing to save? You may know all this, and be lost for ever. But, are you born again? Are you a partaker of a new nature? a divine nature? Are you an heir of God? Is your standing now in Christ, or in Adam?

Before I can see the kingdom of God, I must have the nature implanted that belongs to that kingdom. This is something more than a mere thought of sin forgiven, or righteousness obtained. It is a question of capacity, of fitness to enjoy, of likeness of nature. What an awful thought, that so many religiously-educated people are lost!

What a hell, where the good, decent, religious sons of Adam have to be for ever shut up with the profane, and the drunkard, and the abominable, and the unclean!

Reader, I entreat of you, think. Think for a moment, did the Lord Jesus speak truth or falsehood? If He spoke truth, those who have not *been born again*, however intelligent, educated, moral, benevolent, or religious, can never see the kingdom of God, and must, therefore, be swept away for ever with the lost, for there are only two places. What a hell! Frequenters of places of worship, and frequenters of gin-palaces, tract-distributors and pick-pockets, drawing-room meeting religionists and the offscourings of the streets! Priests who, with solemn mien, pretended to stand between the people and God, and murderers who have been hanged for their crimes! Teachers who knew everything in theology, and the profane, the swearer, the blasphemer, the infidel! These things will turn out true whether you believe them or not. It was seen in the days of Noah. Is it to be your bitter experience? Hell is real. Eternal punishment is real. Christ's words are true, although they may be doubted or denied by the majority of men. The awful fact remains. Stop, therefore, high or low, rich or poor, educated or uneducated, intelligent or ignorant, religious man or blasphemer, respectable or profane; think, and ask yourself these questions, *Am I born again? Have I a new life?*—a life communicated by the Spirit of God through the truth—born not of

flesh, but of water (the word, Eph. v. [...]
Spirit. *Have I been born twice?*—[...]
world of Adam, and again into the [...]
God? Friend, if you have not this new b[...]
better that you had never been born. [...]
as you are, and where you are, if you [...]
vinced of the necessity of this new birth, [...]
live; believe and be saved; take God at [...]
He says, 'Ye *must* be born again; a[...]
same chapter it is written, 'As Moses [...]
the serpent in the wilderness, even so [...]
Son of Man be lifted up, that whosoever [...]
ETH on Him should not perish, but have [...]
LIFE.'—What God demands, God provide[...]

IV.—HOW THE NEW NATURE IS IMPLAN[TED]

This new nature is not implanted by a p[...]
but received by an act of faith. This new [...]
never sets aside as to actual fact the old; [...]
amalgamates, never becomes incorporated w[...]
never improves it, but 'lusts' against it [...]
believer, wars against it, is 'contrary' t[...]
And how is it implanted? Reader, this is of [...]
greatest importance to you. Are you to look [...]
the new birth in your own frames or feeli[...]
to an ordinance or an act of man? A mist[...]
here is fatal—" Ye must be born again."—Ho[...]

The Lord answers this, and gives us the th[...]
things that are divinely and absolutely essen[...]
for the new birth (John iii. 7,) for seeing the ki[...]
dom, (ver. 3,) entering the kingdom, (ver. 5,) [...]
having eternal life, (ver. 15,) all these being [...]

different aspects of the same truth. These three essentials are—
1. Water, (ver. 5.)
2. The Spirit, (vers. 5 and 8.)
3. The Son of Man lifted up, (ver. 14.)
Let us consider each shortly:—

I.—WATER.

'Except a man be born of WATER and of the Spirit, he cannot enter the kingdom of God' (ver. 5.)

It cannot in any way refer to baptism by water, the application of literal water to a man externally, as that would only wash his body, and could not touch his inner man. Some would read the text, 'except a man be born of baptism,' and of course by this doctrine Old Testament saints could not be in the kingdom of God, as they were not baptised. Circumcision could not save a man. 'Neither is that circumcision which is outward in the flesh. . . . Circumcision is that of the heart in the spirit, and not in the letter' (Rom. ii. 28, 29.) No change on a man externally can profit. He may apply much nitre, and wash himself with much soap, but his leopard spots of sin still remain. Nor will mere education, reformation, cultivation, training of the old nature, turn flesh into spirit. 'That which is born of the flesh is flesh;' it may be decent or indecent flesh, religious or irreligious, pious or profane, but still it is flesh.

Some seeing this and understanding it, have

now asked, what can the 'water [...]
has been answered in several ways [...]
is the same as the Spirit, others [...]
same as the blood, but 'there are th[ree]
witness, the Spirit, and the water, an[d the blood]
so that if water were only another w[ay of express-]
ing either the working of the Sp[irit or the]
cleansing of the blood, there would b[e but two]
bearing testimony—the Spirit and th[e blood,]
the water standing for either. We ca[n answer the]
question by asking what should have [been in]
the mind of Nicodemus when Chris[t spoke of]
water? He, a master of Israel, knew [of the laver]
where every priest had to wash befor[e he could]
enter into the holy place, for no unwa[shed man]
ever trod that holy place. He, a master [in Israel,]
knew the book of Ezekiel, and the prom[ise to be]
fulfilled in a coming day to Israel. 'Th[en will I]
sprinkle clean *water* upon you, and ye [shall be]
clean: from all your filthiness and from [all your]
idols will I cleanse you. A new heart a[lso will]
I give you, and a new spirit will I put [within]
you. ... And I will put my Spirit with[in you,]
and cause you to walk in My *statutes*; and [ye shall]
keep My judgments and do *them*.' (Ezek[iel xxxvi.]
25, 26, 27.)

A teacher in Israel should have been lo[oking]
for the antitype of temple and laver, and th[e]
water of purification sprinkled to cleanse fr[om de-]
filement. He should have been conversan[t with]
the 119th Psalm, which definitely explain[s what]
the water is: (ver. 9,) 'Wherewithal sh[all]

young man *cleanse* his way? by taking heed according to Thy *word*.'

The water here spoken of by Christ, and typified in the Old Testament, is the WORD OF GOD, the embodiment, the revelation of God's thoughts.

Let us search the Scriptures as to this: 'Being born again, not of corruptible seed, but of incorruptible, by the *Word of God*, which liveth and abideth for ever. For all flesh is as grass' (1 Pet. i. 23.) In our text 'flesh' is contrasted with the 'spirit,' here flesh is contrasted with the 'Word.' 'The seed is the *Word of God*' (Luke viii. 11). 'The righteousness which is of faith speaketh on this wise, . . . The *Word* is nigh thee' (Rom. x. 6-8.) 'Of His own will begat He us with *the Word* of truth' (James i. 18). 'Ye are *clean* through *the Word* which I have spoken unto you' (John xv. 3).

These all show that 'THE WORD' is used in other parts of Scripture which treat of the new birth in that place where Christ speaks of 'WATER' to Nicodemus, but we have more direct evidence in Eph. v. 26, 'That He might sanctify and cleanse it (the Church) with the washing of water by *the Word*.' Thus, from Old Testament type, from New Testament analogy, and from direct scriptural statement in both Old and New Testaments, the *water* in the new birth is proved to be the '*Word of God*.'

And most important it is to see this. How am I born again by *the Word?* Water cleanses by displacement. Uncleanness and water cannot occupy the same space at the same moment; the

water displaces the uncleanness, and
The Word of God does not act by the
flesh,' but by displacing all the thoughts
flesh' and putting in those of God.

The entrance of God's word gives light
cxix. 130). Man was lost by hearing
is saved by hearing God. Man, in his
Adam-standing, is a chaos—nothing to
meet or please the eye of God—he is without
and void, darkness brooding over him
God therefore begins to re-create him,
are *His* workmanship, *created* in Christ
unto good works,' Eph. ii. 10,) He says
light be,' and light is; and it is by the
of His word that this is done.

This word of God judges everything in
it puts God and His requirements before
Human opinion is entirely set aside. By it
we are all apt to rest satisfied that there are
worse than we. 'If I am lost, many will have
bad chance,' is sometimes said, and quite true
God's Word tells us we are all guilty; and,
saw in a former chapter, 'there is no difference
all are condemned already, equally condemned
compare ourselves with one another, or judge
selves according as men are estimated, bad, good
or indifferent. God's Word comes like water,
washes out all our thoughts and opinions.

'It's my idea,' says one, 'if one tries to live
good life, this is all he can do.' Of course,
is your idea, but all our thoughts are evil, and
God's Word displaces our ideas we are undone

'*Ye must be Born Again!*'

'It's my opinion,' says another, 'that we must just do the best we can, and trust in the mercy of God.' Of course this is your opinion—but the action of God's Word is like water to wash out our opinions. The first thing it tells me about man is that he is lost, depraved, guilty, condemned.

But more; the Word of God brings in God's mind about Himself instead of my own; it lets God think for me, God speak for me, God act for me; it makes me passive, because I can be nothing else.

'*Hear*, and your soul shall live' (Isa. lv. 3). Life is on its syllables—man begins to speak, to pray, &c., when he wants to be saved—God says, *Hear!* God is beseeching you to be reconciled to Him, and should we not answer this gracious beseeching of God before we begin to try to pray? He does beseech men by us (2 Cor v. 20). His prayer is easily answered. He says, 'Will you have my Son?' and the answer is '*Yes*' or '*No*.' By thus hearing the Word of God, and understanding it, (Matt. xiii. 23,) we receive a new life from God, in which God's thoughts reside, and in which they act. Let us now look at the Spirit's work in regeneration.

2.—THE SPIRIT.

We must be born of the SPIRIT—not the Spirit apart from the Word—not the Word apart from the Spirit—not two births—but the one divine new birth. We see Spirit and Word as the *living*

D

water; (John vii. 38). 'He that [believeth on] me, as the Scripture hath said, out [of him] shall flow rivers of living water. B[ut spake] He of the Spirit, which they that beli[eve] should receive.' This was seen at Pen[tecost;] the rivers of living water (read Peter['s sermon] which has so many Old Testament qu[otations] flowed out to the salvation of thousands, [Word] of God carried home by the Spirit—he[re is the] water; the Word is the water, but it is [dry] or dead without the Spirit—Spirit and W[ord,] *living water.* Again, our Lord said, (John [vi. 63)] 'The *words* that I speak unto you they a[re spirit] and they are life.' Mere moral suasion, [so] called, never yet saved a man. This W[ord] operates as God's Spirit applies it. The [vessel] is the Word, but the power is the Spirit.

If people are famishing in a town, and [we in-] tend to send supplies to them, we load [trucks] and waggons with bread and corn, and m[ake] a large train. The entrance of these wagg[ons will] bring life to many a famished family, to m[any a] dying man. Why delay, then? why is th[e train] lying useless at this station where there is pl[enty?] We are waiting for that powerful engine [that] will speed it along. Screw up the coupling; [make] all fast; and now not only is the feast read[y, but] feast and guests are brought together. C[hrist] Himself is the bread, the Word is the wa[ggon,] and the Spirit is the engine or power that b[rings] Christ in the Word to us poor perishing sinn[ers.]

God made a great feast, and bade many (L[uke]

xiv. 16); none came, and 'none of those men which were bidden shall taste of my supper,' is now what God has said. No merely invited guest ever came. We preach 'Come,' we tell that all things are ready, that the feast is spread, the door open, that 'yet there is room;' but no man by this mere invitation ever came; as one has said, 'God has to fill the chairs, as well as the table.' Five yoke of oxen or a piece of ground are of much more value to a natural man than the richest feast of God. God has to provide the guests as well as the feast. If there were no Christ provided, there would be no feast; if there were no Spirit working, there would be no guests.

Ye must be born of the Spirit. Like produces like. 'That which is born of the flesh' is not merely like 'the flesh,' but is 'flesh,' and 'that which is born of the Spirit' is not merely like the Spirit, nor is it the Spirit, (that would be incarnation,) but 'is spirit,' and He dwells in that which He begets.

This is something quite different from 'the flesh' being pardoned, then taught, then toned down, pervaded, and sanctified, by the Spirit. We have the man, the I, the existing person with undivided responsibility, '*born again*' by the thoughts of God acting in him in power, and the mind and nature of God communicated to him by the Spirit; and this now is the man's life, as the 'flesh' was his life before. No Christian can have his standing 'in the flesh.' Alas, that ever any of us should walk in the flesh: 'we are not in the flesh;' alas, the flesh is in us still.

A boat has been sailing on the [...]
come through many a storm, and [...]
briny water, it is now sailing on [...]
of the river. It is no longer in the [...]
the salt water is in it. The Christian [...]
the Adam-sea for ever. He is in the [...]
for ever. Adam is still in him, which [...]
mortify and to throw out, but he is not [...]
He has now a power, and a position, [...]
tion to judge himself. He knows h[...]
was at this point that Paul exclaimed, [...]
that in me—that is, in my flesh—dwell[...]
good thing.' He is not two persons, but [...]
one person he has, and will have to his l[...]
here, two natures diametrically oppos[...]
actively opposing each other. He now s[...]
'the flesh' lusts against the 'Spirit,' b[...]
Spirit also against the 'flesh,' in order t[...]
may not walk as he used to walk; that th[...]
contrary, and therefore never can be friend[...]
that he has in him, and will have in him[...]
that is neither to be trifled with nor trusted[...]
watched, warred with, and mortified.

Christ is now his life. He is now a 'par[...]
of the divine nature,' 'born of God,' 'an h[...]
God;' and thus it is with every one who is [...]
of the Spirit, Jew or Gentile, for God acts h[...]
sovereignty. Connection with Abraham only [...]
them a fleshly standing, but a new thing is no[...]
by the Jew as well as the Gentile, and is as [...]
to the Gentile as to the Jew.

The eighth verse of John iii. is a most bl[...]

verse. Here we heathen sinners of the Gentiles have got in. Reader, never quarrel with the royal prerogative of God's grace; read Rom. ix., and see that if we do not let God be absolute we have no chance of salvation, for we are all equally 'condemned already.' Praise His grace that hath now appeared to every nation under heaven.

But passing over Christ's testimony of the Father as given in verses nine to thirteen—(prophets had prophesied, but here is *God Himself*)—let us now look at

3.—THE SON OF MAN LIFTED UP.

This, indeed, is our life. Christ said, 'Ye MUST be born again;' but here is another MUST that He mentions, 'As Moses lifted up the serpent in the wilderness, even so MUST the Son of Man be lifted up: that whosoever believeth on Him should not perish but have everlasting life.' God says, 'Ye *must*,' but He also says, 'I *must*.' Your Adam-life is forfeited, and you are under condemnation. The Son of Man lifted up is the answer to the forfeit. Satan, who has the power of death, and has every man in his power (for all have sinned), has been destroyed as to his power, his head having been bruised by Christ on the cross. (Heb. ii. 14.) But Christ is now risen, and can communicate His life to any one who believes in Him, He having satisfied every demand of God. The new birth is the communication of a new life. Christ beyond the doom of sin is that life; Christ incarnate before His death cannot be 'our life,' because the judgment against the old life can only be met in *death*.

The 'corn of wheat' *must* die before the fruit can be produced. The life of Christ raised from the dead is therefore the new life preached to the *sinner*, and implanted in him on his *believing*—a life that is perfect, impeccable, indestructible, eternal as the Christ of God—a life that has already proved victorious over the cross of shame, over death's strongest power—a life that will ere long swallow up mortality.

The Spirit of God applies the Word that speaks about the lifted-up Christ whom we receive and rest upon for salvation, and this is the new birth. Such a life is offered only to a *sinner*—what a comfort! No righteous man, no earth-wise, no rich man, ever entered the kingdom of God as such—but only as justified sinners. None but *redeemed* sinners sing the song of that kingdom —none but those who, guilty, depraved, lost, have taken their place with roused consciences at the foot of the cross, and there have seen the lifted-up Christ. All in that kingdom are '*new creatures*,' clothed in 'the best robe,' with the 'ring,' and the 'shoe,' and 'the fatted calf' slain. What perfection is in the Word of God! The Word tells me that unless I am born again I cannot enter God's kingdom; but the same Word tells me that if I am born again, though only a babe now, I am as sure of spending eternity with my Lord as if I were already with Him. No hatred of devils, no enmity of the world, no power of the flesh, shall keep me out. We enter God's kingdom by being born again. We *have* eternal life even now. We have the germs of heaven even here. We do not wait for that life; but 'he that believeth on the Son HATH everlasting life' (ver. 36).

We have tried to shew thus briefly what is meant by being 'born of water and of the Spirit.' Read 1 John v. 6—'This is He that came by water and blood, not by water only, but by water and blood, and it is the Spirit that beareth witness, because the Spirit is truth. For they that bear witness are three; the *Spirit*, and the *water*, and the *blood*, and the three agree in one.' (Correct translation.)

The *blood* is for expiation; that is, the Son of man lifted-up on the cross, and his life taken for ours. 'This is He that came by water and blood' (1 John v. 6).

The *water* is for cleansing; that is, the Word of God applied in power to our consciences. Christ 'came not by water only' (that is to say, not merely a teacher of the word), 'but by water and blood.' He came certainly as the great teacher, but also as the great sacrifice making atonement for sin.

The *Spirit* is the witness from the throne of God to the value of that blood in the presence of God, and the witness to our spirits by applying the word (water), and thus morally cleansing. He is also the source, the framer, and the power of expression of every new feeling, thought, affection, or purpose in the new creation, 'and it is the Spirit that beareth witness, because the Spirit is truth.'

These three agree in one, meet in one point, work out one thing in their testimony, and this is the testimony, that 'God hath given to us eternal life, and this life is in His Son. He that hath the Son, hath life' (1 John v. 11, 12).

What the sinner, therefore, has to do in this new birth is to look to Christ on the cross; and where is he to look to Him now as crucified but in *the Word*? He is to believe what God says about His Son. God says, I have given you Christ (John iii. 16). I believe it: therefore I thank God. I do not ask myself do I feel it? but God says it—I appropriate Christ as mine—I believe His Word, by putting in my name where God puts His 'whosoever.' In this Word of God we get the Spirit's witness—that is, God's testimony about His Son. God does the *work:* we believe the *Word*.

Reader, are you *born again?* You are not satisfied with yourself. Nor is God satisfied with you. You are not satisfied with your estimate of the work of Christ. Are you satisfied with God's estimate of it? The Spirit has come to tell out to us the value of that blood. Faith does not consist in my valuing it, but in my accepting God's value of it. God says, 'When I see the blood, I will pass over you.'

If you do not believe God's witness, the Spirit of God in the Word, about His Son, you simply make God a liar. Now you must either make yourself a liar, or God. Do you not think that it would be the better way to say, 'Let God be true and *every* man a liar'—myself the first liar? A man does not like to be called a liar, but God says, 'every man.' Until a man calls himself a liar, he makes God one. 'He that believeth not God hath made Him a liar, because he believeth not the record that God gave of His Son. And this is the record, that God hath given to us eternal life, and this life is in His Son.' As long as you look within yourself for one idea, one opinion, one thought, you are listening to a liar. Call your heart a liar at once and simply take God at His word, receive His Son as He has given Him to you.

Reader, art *thou* born again? There was a moment that every Israelite had between being bitten and dying; that moment was given him to look and LIVE. That is thy brief moment of life; hast thou looked and lived? God can do no more than He has done to provide life for thee. He spared not His Son?

Do not look to thy wounds, to thy sins, and think thus to get peace. Try no longer earth's prayers, or religions, or works of righteousness: they are but ointments to thy sores, that will never heal: but look away from all to the serpent on the pole. The question is not, whether thou hast great faith or little faith. It did not depend upon the length of the look, nor the earnestness of the look, it was the fact of looking that cured the bitten Israelite. Look and live! thou hast only one brief yet sufficient moment of time.

But how are men spending this little moment? In making money, in indulging the lust of the flesh, the lust of the eye, and the pride of life! In gathering together the dust of their condemned cell into heaps, and calling it riches! In gathering the straws that lie in their prison, and making crowns, and madman-like, playing at kings, while death is written as their doom; and the door of escape stands still open!

God is standing over them with this awful word of truth, 'YE MUST BE BORN AGAIN,' and this precious word of grace, 'THE SON OF MAN MUST BE LIFTED UP.' He delivered up His Son to death. What a holy God! What a just, righteous, truthful God! When sin was lying on the sinless Christ, He could not let it pass. Do you think He will let *you* pass now after that awful day at Calvary? It is there that we read the doom of sin. How shall we escape from Him if we neglect His 'so great salvation?' For it is not merely with God as a judge we have to do; it was His *love* that planned and wrought the whole redemption work. Doubly bitter will be your cup of wrath that you have spurned the salvation of such a God who desires to be known by you as LOVE; for in order that *any* poor sinner might be born again, '*God so loved the* WORLD *that He gave His only-begotten Son, that* WHOSOEVER *believeth on Him should not perish, but have everlasting life.*' (John iii. 16.)

'*Ye must be Born Again.*'

Let us suppose that you are convinced of these important realities—that you are lost, that therefore your first need is a *Saviour*, not a *teacher*; that you have not a nature capable of enjoying God; that the new nature is gotten by your being born—born again of water (the word) and the Spirit, but you cannot understand how this comes about. You cannot understand what is meant by looking to Christ as the bitten Israelites looked to the serpent on the pole. Let me illustrate it by a conversation I had, one day, with a man who had been hearing the gospel preached, and with whom I had to walk some miles.

I began by asking, 'Have you ever thought of the great salvation?'

'O yes,' he replied, 'I have often thought about it.'

'And are you saved?'

'Well I could not say that—I don't feel as I would like.'

'I quite believe that; but do you think any of us could ever feel perfectly right in this world? But are you at peace with God?'

'I never could say that I was satisfied with myself.'

'But, my friend, I did not ask if you were. It would be a very bad sign if you were satisfied with yourself. But are you at peace with God?'

'Well, I never could feel that I had peace.'

'But I don't ask if you feel at peace with yourself; I hope you never will. Have you peace with God?'

'To tell you the truth, I am n[ot].'

'How long is it since you b[egan] these things?'

'About seven or eight years ago[, in] of Ireland, I was first awakened b[y] preaching on "*Ye must be born ag[ain]*" often since that time I have been t[rying] God's Spirit working in me.'

'And you never have?'

'No; I could not be sure.'

'How could ever any one be sure o[f what is] going on within him, especially as [Satan] comes as an angel of light?'

'Well, what am I to do, then?'

'The Lord Jesus was the one, you [know,] that said, "Ye must be born again." "[Except a] man be born of water and of the Spirit, h[e cannot] enter the kingdom of God." Now, at th[e end of] all this conversation, Nicodemus did no[t know] how to be saved, but only said, "How ca[n these] things be?" even when the Lord Himself [was his] great Teacher.'

'That's just where I am.'

'Now, what did the Lord do? He too[k him] away to the picture-book for children, and s[howed] him the picture of a dying man looking [away] from himself to a serpent on a pole, and [so] obtaining life; and told him that "as [Moses] lifted up the serpent in the wilderness, even so [must] the Son of Man be lifted up, that whosoev[er be-] lieveth in Him should not perish, but have et[ernal] life." Now all you have to do is to look and li[ve.]

'But that is just what I've been trying to do, and what I don't know how to do :—what is it to look to Christ?'

'Now I can understand your difficulty; you cannot see Christ with the eyes of your body; you cannot see Him in vision; you say that you cannot feel His presence within you; you cannot feel that you have faith.'

'Exactly; what am I to do?'

'Allow me to give you an illustration.' In some such words I spoke with my friend, and gave him the substance of the following illustration, which seemed to clear away his difficulty; and I trust, by God's blessing, it may enable you to receive God's simple plan, and accept God's salvation for nothing.

You have a rent—say £10 a-year—to pay. Having to maintain a large family, and having been recently in distress and out of work, you find it impossible to pay it. Let us suppose that I was able, knew your difficulty, took pity on you, and said to you—

John, I hear you have your rent coming on, and having had very hard times, you will never be able to pay it. Now I wish you to use your money for your most pressing wants, to get food and clothing for your wife and family, and *look to me for the rent*. You, knowing me, and hence believing me, would go away home with a burden off your mind and a happy heart. When you came home next Saturday with your wages, you would tell your wife to spend all the money in getting food and clothing.

'But, John,' she would say, 'are we not to lay aside something for the rent?'

'Oh no,' you would answer; 'I met a man whom I know, and he said, *Look to me for the rent*, and I believe him.'

And thus weeks would go on, till shortly before the rent-day a neighbour comes in and says—

'John, I have only got £5 gathered for my rent, and I don't know what I'm to do. How much have you?'

'None at all.'

'What! have you nothing gathered?'

'No, for a friend of mine said, *Look to me for the rent*.'

'And are you not getting anxious about it?'

'No.'

'Why?'

'Because I *trust* him.'

'Why?'

'Because I *believe* him.'

'Why?'

'Because I *know* him.'

By and by the rent-day comes, and even your wife begins to be suspicious and doubtful, but you have implicit trust in what I said—you have no difficulty in understanding what *look to me for the rent* means; and so, at the appointed hour, I walk in and make my word good, and am happy to find that, against all your neighbour's doubts, against all your wife's fears, and even against all your own tremblings, you have trusted my word and looked to me for the rent.

'This is, of course, just an illustration, as I have no doubt you are at the present quite able and willing to pay your own rent; but in the matter of our salvation, though we might be willing, we are totally unable; so the Lord now says, 'Look to Me, and be ye saved.'

Christ on the cross has satisfied God's justice. He paid the debt for the sinner. Men are doing perfectly right things; praying, living moral lives, and giving money for charitable purposes, but all for the wrong end. All these will never save. God says, '*Look to Me for salvation*,' and then begin to use your time, talents, money, powers, for their legitimate end, to glorify God. Do not try to be holy in order to be saved. That would be like the man laying up for a rent which he could never pay. '*Look to Me and be saved*,' says God, and then be holy, because you are sure of salvation on the authority of God. Religion will never save you—even pure religion. God defines pure religion in James i. 27 : ' Pure religion, and undefiled, before God and the Father is this, to visit the fatherless and widows in their affliction, and to keep himself unspotted from the world.' By the deeds of the law we cannot be justified; therefore by doing all this we cannot be saved. Religion is the life of a saved man, not the efforts of an unsaved man to get saved. We do not try to do good in order to get a new nature, but we try to do good because we have received a new nature. The work which God will accept from you is not *to* the cross, it is *from* the cross to the crown. Christ did ALL the *saving-work*. He brought the cross to our level. Be saved by looking to Him, and then live to God. Do not look to the feeling of being saved—look away from what is being wrought *in* you to what was wrought *for* you. We are not saved on account of the Spirit working in us, but by means of His work—we are saved on account of Christ dying for us. We are not saved *for* faith but *through* faith. 'Look to me and be ye saved, all the ends of the earth.'

Lie down as a wounded, helpless, ungodly sinner, and look away from yourself to Christ crucified for sin.

> *Look unto Me and be ye saved—*
>   Look, men of nations all;
> Look rich and poor, look old and young,—
>   Look sinners great and small!
>
> *Look unto Me and be ye saved—*
>   Look now, nor dare delay;
> Look as you are—lost, guilty, dead—
>   Look while 'tis called to-day!
>
> *Look unto Me and be ye saved—*
>   Look from your doubts and fears;
> Look from your sins of crimson dye,
>   Look from your prayers and tears!
>
> *Look unto Me and be ye saved—*
>   Look to the work all done,
> Look to the pierced Son of Man,
>   Look to your sin all gone!

Do you feel your Sins forgiven?
OUR ASSURANCE.

'DO you *feel* that your sins are all forgiven?'
'Indeed I do not; but I *know* they are.'
'Now, I cannot understand that. How can any one know it?'
'If you had wronged me, and I told you that I forgave you, would you not know it?'
'Most certainly; but how can you say that God ever told you that He forgave you? Did you just feel at a certain time something that you thought was God's voice, inwardly telling you that your sins were pardoned?'
'I certainly did not.'
'Then how can it be? I have tried to get converted as hard as any man could; I have prayed for grace, for strength, for the pardon of my sins, and for the Holy Spirit, and I do not yet feel any difference, and I never could feel as I have heard some men say they felt.'
'I quite understand you; I was for years in the same condition.'
'Then how did you get out of it? I know all about the plan of salvation, about the work of Christ, and the necessity of the Spirit; that we must be justified by grace through faith alone

without the works of the law; [...]
are all most certainly secure to [...]
Christ; but how am I ever to k[now]
am in Him or not?'

'I know that you may have heard [Chris-]
tians say they *feel* they are pardon[ed,]
they are saved; but this only tends [to...]
It did mislead me, and I have no doub[t is]
leading you. These Christians may m[ean the right]
thing, but they state it wrongly. I [say it is]
because I *know* that my sins are pard[oned.]
I will show you how I know that by[e and bye,]
but I do not *feel* that my sins are [pardoned.]
Let us suppose a case. A poor wido[w has no]
money to pay her debts. The credito[r is de-]
manding his righteous due. A friend [steps in]
and says to the creditor, "I'll pay you the [widow's]
debt;" he puts down the money, and the [credi-]
tor hands him a slip of paper on which is w[ritten]
"Received from Widow Blank the sum [of £—]
settled," with the creditor's signature [attached.]
The receipt is handed to the widow, and sh[e is]
very happy *because* she knows that her d[ebt is]
paid. If you were to call that day, and [ask]
the widow, "Do you *feel* that your debt is p[aid?"]
what would she say?'

'Feel it! What do you mean? There i[s the]
receipted account. I don't feel that it's paid[, but]
I *feel* very happy *because it is paid*.'

'Now, do you not see the difference? Tha[t feel-]
ing is all right, but I do not feel my sin pardon[ed,]
I know it, and hence feel happy.'

'But does it not say somewhere in Scripture that the Spirit beareth witness with our spirits?'

'Now from the very fact that you speak so vaguely about "somewhere in Scripture," I fear that you do not know well what Scripture is. The Bible is not a number of texts strung together at random: it is a perfectly arranged whole. Truth in a wrong connexion is the worst kind of error. You find in Romans viii. 16, this most blessed and wondrous revelation from God, that "The Spirit itself beareth witness with our spirits, that we are the children of God." Mark carefully, this is not given as a ground by which to know that our sins are forgiven; but comes after the whole revelation of the truth concerning what we have done and what we are, and how our responsibilities are met. It comes after the triumphant assertion of Romans v. 1, "Being justified by faith we have peace with God," and that crowning triumph after every question has been settled against us, "There is no condemnation." (Rom. viii. 1.) At peace with God, and no condemnation, we now advance into our peculiar place among the creatures of God. Angels are at peace with God and have no condemnation, but they have not the standing that we have. Here is something additional, "We are the children of God; and if children then heirs, heirs of God and joint-heirs with Christ." Angels are called sons in Job i. 6, and other Scriptures. They are the highest unfallen creatures, and man was made a little lower than they, but is now made higher

than they in virtue of redemp...
They are kept by God's power...
without variableness or shadow of...
Christ is the same yesterday, to-...
ever. We are fellow heirs with...
anew in Christ Jesus our responsib...
this is our security.

'Being taken from the swine-trough...
ting food and raiment, we would th...
content, glad that we were in the ho...
even among the servants. But higher...
vants are we become, even heirs. We...
pause, and say, is this presumption?...
say that all things are mine? that I a...
a son, an heir of God? Yes! indeed...
the Spirit has been sent to dwell with us...
be in us, as coming from the throne rev...
our spirit (which can now discern spiritual...
that, without presumption, we may lay...
the title, the relationship, of son of God,...
God, and joint-heir with Christ. That Sp...
within every believer, and seals only saved...
He quickens the unsaved. God has sent...
this testimony, and he that is a believer h...
'testimony in himself' (1 John v. 10). Th...
portant point I wish you to see is this, that...
Holy Ghost is never said to bear witness...
by any internal feeling, that we are at peace...
God. It is after a man knows he is a s...
man that then there is a step further...
him—namely, that he is a son and hei...
Christ. He is not only out of prison: he i...

at the table of the King whom he calls "Abba," that is, Father.'

'I quite understand the distinction, but I never saw it before; but if I could know that I was at peace with God I would be quite satisfied.'

'Yes, but God would not; however, this is the first point for you to know—"being justified by *faith* we have peace with God," not by the *feeling* of faith.'

'But don't some people feel it, while others do not?'

'Not at all. What I am contending for is that the forgiveness of sins is a thing that can be felt by no one: and, unless the knowledge of it is founded on the Word of God, and that alone, for every one, individually, it will be sinking sand for a deathbed. Scores of anxious people have been deluded into the idea that they knew the gospel when some pleasing emotion passed through their minds. When Satan sees people awakened, and that he cannot keep them quiet, he takes his stand beside the preacher of the gospel, and while he is inviting them to the rock, Satan pushes out planks of feeling. A drowning man will catch at a straw, and the poor troubled one finds a little relief in resting on some plank of quietness of conscience, till storms rage, and then he finds himself with nothing beneath him. I am therefore suspicious when a person tells me he is "a little better." If he does not believe the gospel, he has no right to be any better, and if he has taken the good news to himself, he is entitled to be at perfect peace.

'Then you don't allow of any feeling?'

'Most certainly I do: but what am I warranted in feeling? If I could tell you that you were saved, and you believed it, would you not feel happy?'

'Of course I would.'

'This is what I feel — whenever I say to myself, "I'm saved," don't I feel happy? and the more I realise that my knowledge of salvation depends only on God's word, the more happy I become?'

'Is there nothing about this "feeling saved" in the Bible?'

'Indeed, there is not. You can easily satisfy yourself by turning to a concordance. Never once is the word put beside "salvation," "forgiveness," or, in fact, anything about a man's peace with God, but we find in Luke i. 77, that part of John's commission is declared to be "to give KNOWLEDGE of salvation," and in many parts of Scripture we find "knowing our sins forgiven," "knowing Whom we have believed," "knowing we have passed from death to life," "knowing we are born of God." Did Abraham feel he was to have a son when he was so old? No! but he knew it. And how did he know it? Because God said it. He felt glad because he knew it, because he believed what God said. It is really because people do not believe that God means exactly what He says, that we see so many intelligent men who cannot say whether they are saved or not.'

'But I have often thought that I had received Christ and trusted in Him alone; yet I find my faith so incapable of producing effects.'

'But did you start saying "I'm saved," before trying to do anything?'

'O no! I was always waiting for fruits.'

'Fruits of what? fruits of doubt? Suppose you had got the right fruits, would you then have believed you were saved?'

'O yes!'

'That is to say, you would trust the fruits you brought forth rather than God's word—not for your salvation, but for your knowledge of it. But you must be saved, and know you are saved, before one acceptable fruit can be brought forth—else the works are legal. All evangelical obedience is rendered by a man who is saved, and who renders it because he knows that he is saved.'

'Then am I to do nothing?'

'Absolutely and literally nothing. You must take salvation exactly as the thief on the cross did. He could not turn over a new leaf; his last wretched leaf had been turned in reviling his Saviour. He could not do any work for God, for there was a nail through each hand; he could not run in the way of God's commandments, for there was a nail through his feet. And until you stand still and realize that there is a nail through all your self-righting activity, and a nail through all your carnal agility, and accept salvation for nothing, knowing that you are saved simply on the authority of the bare Word of God, you will never be saved. We do not look inward to what we feel, nor outward to what we do—but to the Son of Man lifted up, and to God's account of how well He is pleased with the Lord Jesus Christ.'

'Well, I think I see what you mean, and it clears up a real difficulty. I am not to examine myself to see if I *feel* better, *feel* saved, *feel* forgiven, or *feel* happy; but here is the next difficulty—how am I to know it?'

'I well remember that when I began trying to feel converted, I felt myself becoming worse and worse, and my heart getting further and further from peace. Then I began to study this and that theological question. I knew all about what Calvinism and Arminianism were—studied my Bible till I knew its contents pretty well; but at last I found I was not on the right track for salvation at all. I was thinking that salvation came *intellect-wise*, and not *faith-wise*.'

'But a man cannot be saved apart from his understanding?'

'Most certainly not, no more than he can be saved against his will; but the eyes of his understanding must be enlightened, that he may be made willing to receive the gift of salvation in God's way. You see if God had made His salvation dependent upon education or intellect, He would have left the great mass without the chance of salvation until they were tutored up to the requisite point; but as there is *one salvation* for high and low, rich and poor, educated and ignorant, so there is *one method* of receiving it, and of course that must be according to the standard of the most unlearned. Hence the truth of the remark that a friend made to me, "Intellect never helped me to Christ, but it often hindered me."

'I was trying to explain this (which I believe to be of the greatest importance) to some poor people, and I tried to illustrate it in this way. If, in travelling by rail, I had a first-class ticket, I could travel one part of the journey in a first-class carriage, another part in a second, and another in a third, and the railway officials could find no fault; but, if I had only a third-class ticket, I must remain in the third from beginning to end. Thus, in regard to salvation, the educated man can come to the uneducated man's platform; the uneducated cannot rise to his: therefore it is on the common platform on which ALL men can stand, that God treats concerning salvation.

'This is the great difficulty; this is why not many great, not many wise, and not many noble, can afford to come low enough among the common run of people, to take a guilty sinner's place, receive a lost sinner's Saviour, and rejoice in a condemned sinner's pardon. This is why Christ taught that men had to become like little children before they could get into the kingdom of heaven.'

'I see the justice of your remarks; but tell

me, now, how am I to get into the Kingdom?'

'As you have said before, you know that it is *of grace*—that is to say, God is waiting to give it to you *all for nothing*, without a feeling in payment, without a prayer as the condition of it, just as the widow's friend dealt with her debt. That it might be of grace, it was made to be by *faith*, not by *attainment* either in intellect or feeling. This is the impression that has been sometimes left upon my mind, after having heard the gospel stated — that faith is the condition which God has demanded from the sinner, in order that he may be saved — that the great Physician will heal the most wretched sin-burdened soul, but He must receive faith as his *fee!* Now this, as you have no doubt found, would be the most difficult of all fees to procure. Feeling is hard to get up, but faith is harder. Faith is the mere apprehension of grace—thankfully accepting what God has already freely given. Faith puts God in the chief room as the giver, it being more blessed to give than to receive, and lets Him do everything, man being the silent and passive receiver of blessing. Faith has to do, not with what I feel toward God, but with what God feels towards me, what He has done for me, and what He has told me. Faith does not look into its own formation—it looks out to God's provided substitute for the sinner. Faith does not tell me to *feel* that I am converted, but it fixes me down to the Word of

God. Faith tells me to take God at His word. Faith has not to do with what I am thinking of myself, bad or good, but it lets God think for me.

'Two things are to be distinguished, "salvation" and the "knowledge of salvation." First, How am I to be saved? and then, How am I to know it?

'First, then, my *salvation* depends solely and entirely upon the work and the *person* of Jesus Christ our Lord. My salvation is supported by His work; His work is supported by His person.

'Secondly, the *knowledge* that I am saved depends solely on the record, the *word*, the testimony of God. "He that believeth not God, hath made Him a liar, because he believeth not the record (testimony) that God gave of His Son." A man is saved the moment he accepts Christ, on account of Christ having died in his place; he knows that he is saved whenever he believes the record that God gave of His Son.'

'Well now, tell me shortly what "believing in the Lord Jesus Christ is." Of course I believe He is able and willing to save anybody, His atonement is sufficient, and His offer free and full; but how is He to become mine?'

'What is it to believe in a man? What is it to believe in a bank? You do not believe in one who is in the black list—but you can look around and say to yourself, "Well, I believe in so and so," and it is just the same with Christ:

I believe in Him—not merely in His historical existence—but I trust Him, I receive, I rest upon Him alone for my salvation.'

'In a word, then, what should I do? I am wishing to take God's way, and willing now to do it. When I begin to go through trains of thought, I get confused, and I should just like to know in a sentence what my path ought to be.'

'*Take the lost sinner's place, and* CLAIM *the lost sinner's Saviour!*'

'Will the claim be allowed?'

'Certainly. For although we are justified *freely* by His grace, still that grace has so planned it, that it puts God in the more blessed place of the giver, and the sinner in the responsible place of the receiver. True it is that he has no claim by nature upon God, but faith uses what grace prescribes. Yea, more, God commands you to claim Him.'

'Can *I* claim Him?'

'Only a lost sinner can.'

'I am allowed, urged, besought, commanded to take Christ as mine; surely I have nothing to lose: yea, Lord, I believe Thee, Christ is mine.'

'I take comfort from the fact that my sins were laid on Christ—I do not *feel* they were there, but God says it—"He was wounded for *our* transgressions;" not for those of angels—they had none; not for those of *devils*—they can claim no Saviour; but for those who take the *sinner's* place: "The chastisement of *our* peace was *upon* Him." Therefore it would be unjust to lay it on me believing on Him. He is a real Saviour for real sinners. My only qualification for such a Saviour is that I am such a sinner. And now I believe my sins are not on me—not because I feel them gone, for I do not, but because God says they were laid on Christ.' (Isaiah liii. 6.)

Robert M'Cheyne says, 'We must not close with Christ because we *feel* Him, but because *God has said it*, and we must take God's word even in the dark.' We do not *feel* we have faith. We accept God's way of dealing with sin.

Man would try to settle God's claims. God Himself has settled the claims, and offers the settled account for nothing. Man would try to make His peace with God. God has come and '*made peace*,' Christ Himself becoming '*our peace*,' and now He is '*preaching peace*' for the acceptance of all (Eph. ii. 14-17). Most anxious enquirers seem to think that we have to fight against ourselves in order to be saved, whereas we fight against ourselves because we are saved. We have a race to run, but it is not *to* the cross, it is *from* the cross. Man's way is to believe *because we feel*: God's way is to feel *because we believe*, and believe because God has said it.

Dr Thomas Chalmers says, 'Yet come the enlargement when it will, it must, I admit, come after all through the channel of a simple credence given to the *sayings of God*, accounted true and

faithful sayings. And never [...]
so fill my heart as when, like [...]
up the lesson that God hath laid [...]
the iniquities of us all.'

*Take the lost sinner's place, and [...]
sinner's Saviour.*

No *works of law* have we to bo[ast],
By nature ruined, guilty, lost,
Condemned already; but Thy hand
Provided what Thou didst demand:
We take the guilty sinner's name,
The guilty sinner's Saviour, claim.

No *faith* we trust. 'Tis Christ alone
'Tis what He is, what He has done,
He is for us as given by God,
It was for us He shed His blood:
We take the guilty sinner's name,
The guilty sinner's Saviour, claim.

We do not *feel* our sins are gone,
But *know* it from Thy word alone:
We know that Thou our sins did'st lay,
On Him who has put sin away:
We take the guilty sinner's name,
The guilty sinner's Saviour, claim.

Because we *know* our sins forgiven,
We happy feel: our home is Heaven.
O help us now as sons, our God,
To tread the path that Christ has trod:
We take the guilty sinner's name,
The guilty sinner's Saviour, claim.

The Work of the Holy Spirit.

OUR COMFORTER.

WE are not saved *on account* of the Holy Ghost's work in us; we are saved *by means of* it. We are saved on account of Christ's work for us. The more the Spirit works within us, the more shall we desire that work to go on; but the work of Christ on Calvary is finished, and this is our resting-place, our peace, our security. Here below we never can (and never should) get satisfied with the work of the Spirit wrought within us; but we are satisfied with the work of Christ done for us, and this is eternal rest, this is faith. Many sadly confuse these two divine works. Anxious inquirers are constantly looking within to see what is going on there, instead of looking outward to what was done on Calvary. I wish to draw the reader's attention to three most precious operations of the Spirit of God as seen in the beginning of John's Gospel—

First, *Born of the Spirit*; chap. iii. 5-8.
Second, *Indwelt by the Spirit*; chap. iv. 14.
Third, *Communicating the Spirit*; chap. vii. 38.

1. BORN OF THE SPIRIT.

Many think that regeneration, or the new birth or quickening, is a process that goes on subsequent to justification. This is a mistake. 'Except a man be born again, he cannot *see* the kingdom of God;' 'He that believeth that Jesus is the Christ is born of God.' Regeneration is an instantaneous act performed by the Spirit of God communicating the life of Christ to a man formerly dead in trespasses and sins, and having nothing whatever in him that could be transformed into this new creation which He implants. There are two errors against which we must guard:

First, not recognising or acknowledging the Spirit's special work in regeneration; and

Second, confusing this with Christ's work done for us.

1st, *It is by a special act of absolute grace that we are born again by the Spirit.* 'The wind bloweth where it listeth,' and so the Jewish Pharisee is compelled to allow God to act as a sovereign. What would be the use of Christ coming, living, dying for sin, rising beyond its doom, and His present intercession, unless the Holy Spirit were here applying to individuals that work, that life by the Word. It is not His influence merely, but Himself, who is now on earth. It is not His Word merely, blessed and essential as it is, but Himself, who applies that Word. Look at the feast in Luke xiv. If Christ had not come and died and risen, there would have been no feast to offer; but if the Holy Spirit were not here, none would come to the feast. So the parable tells us, 'Compel them to come in;' and the Holy Ghost is the great compeller, making them willing. This is His special work on individuals, not His general work in the world. His work on the world is not in the way of *mercy* but of *conviction.*

In John xvi. 8, we read, when He is come He will *reprove* (ελεγξει, literally, *convict by proof* to its confusion) the world—

(1.) '*Of sin,*' because the great sin of which God holds man to be guilty is the crucifixion of His Son ; and the presence of the Holy Ghost is the great proof of man's refusal of Christ, for it is the rejected Christ who has sent the Spirit, and His presence is a continued testimony to that rejection ; hence it is said 'of sin, because they believe not on Me.'

(2.) '*Of righteousness.*' If man is an ungrateful sinner, God is a righteous God who rewards righteously ; and if sinful man gave his Saviour a cross of shame, a righteous God gave His Son a throne of glory. This is the great act of righteousness between God and the man Christ. 'Sit thou at My right hand until I make Thine enemies Thy footstool.' (Ps. cx. 1.) The presence of the Holy Ghost on earth is the proof of the righteousness of God, as also of the righteousness of Christ. In John xvii. our Lord appeals to the righteous Father to judge between Him and the world. He committed Himself to Him that judgeth righteously. Read Psalm xvii., the keynote of which is 'Hear the right.' As the prophetic spirit also said in Isaiah l. 8, ' He is near that justifieth me : who will contend with me ? let us stand together :

who is mine adversary? let him...
Behold, the Lord God will help...
that shall condemn me?' Christ...
glorified God, God glorifies Him...
justice, crowning Him with glory...
And though we see Him not by...
(for Christ is not yet manifested...
throne), yet in the interval between...
triumph, the Father in righteousness...
down on *His* throne, and has sent down...
Ghost to testify that He is glorified;...
is said, 'Of righteousness, because I...
Father, and ye see Me no more.'

(3.) '*Of judgment,*' because, since Sa[tan]...
not hold Christ in death, a power strong[er than]
Satan's must have appeared, whose pow[er in]
death must therefore have been set a[side,]
himself judged, for 'through death He d[estroyed]
Him that had the power of death, that...
devil.' The Holy Ghost has come to te[ll of]
this great act of judgment; because the...
that He has come, proves that Christ h[as died]
and is in glory; and the fact that Chr[ist is]
risen proves that Satan has been judge[d;]
since Satan is the 'prince of this world,' th[en]
has been judged, being set aside in its...
head; therefore it is said, 'Of judgment, b[ecause]
the prince of this world is judged.'

Such is the action of the Holy Ghost...
world to its confusion and shame; but His...
in quickening is quite a distinct thing. He...
not work on 'the old man' in me and ma[ke]

better, and thus gradually save. He shews me that it cannot be mended. He shews me that I am 'guilty,' 'condemned already,' 'lost,' 'alienated,' 'evil only,' 'continually evil,' 'without God,' 'without hope,' 'without strength,' 'dead.'

I have heard men speak of a remaining spark in the bosom of the unregenerate that required merely to be fanned into a flame by the influences of the Holy Ghost. This is unscriptural. (Read Gen. vi. 5, &c.) I have heard such speak of a seed of good in every man which the Holy Ghost cultivates, and this they call the new birth. This is utter confusion, and an entire misconception of the figure. Man's co-operation in regeneration is not required, because he has no power to co-operate. He is dead. 'That which is born of the Spirit is spirit.' The work is altogether of God. As it was God who in His own heart, before the foundation of the world, planned redemption; and as it was God in His Son who, eighteen hundred years ago, before we were born, secured our redemption; so it is God by His Spirit who now, without our endeavour, apart from our effort, applies this redemption. In fact, the first thing God does is *to make us willing*. How entirely is this work of God! He was alone in eternity; He was alone in creation; He was alone in redemption; He is alone in regeneration, which is merely redemption applied. God does not *find* us children; He *makes* us children. But we must look now at another error.

2d. *Confounding the work of the Spirit in us*

with Christ's work for us. While the Spirit of God is the sole agent, the truth of God is the sole instrument which He employs. We cannot see the Spirit; we can see the Word. We cannot see His operations: we can read his record about Christ. No doubt it will be merely letters without meaning, until He opens the eyes; but He works only in His appointed channel. He never tells us to look *inward* even to His own operations, for peace, but *outward to Christ*. That is the most Spirit-honouring preaching of the gospel in which you hear most of Christ. Once I heard a very earnest man preaching to anxious inquirers, and he was dwelling continuously and exclusively upon the Spirit's work—its signs and characteristics—with the effect of confusing many of his hearers. For who could obtain scriptural peace with God from his own feelings? We get a healthful and heaven-born conflict by marking the Holy Ghost's operations within us, but never peace. This we get by gazing at the Lamb of God on Calvary. I thought as I heard the preacher, 'I wonder if the Holy Ghost would preach in that way if He were standing there,' and I immediately remembered, that 'He shall not speak of (from) Himself,' 'He shall testify of Me;' that is, He will preach Christ. 'He shall take of Mine and shall shew it unto you.' 'He shall glorify Me.' This is spiritual preaching, because the preaching of the things of the Spirit, and as He Himself would preach. I believe the more we are depending on the Spirit's working, the more we shall preach what the Spirit wishes us to preach about, and look to Him to apply it. When we begin to point the anxious enquirer to the Spirit's work, this is not how the Spirit Himself would deal with him.

If I began to speak to a working man sitting down to his dinner, and said to him, 'Do you know the muscles employed in mastication?'

'What's that?' he would likely say.

'Well, in eating?'

'Indeed, I do not.'

'And you do not know the nerves that supply them?'

'I'm sure I do not.'

'And the beautiful mechanism and arrangement by which the food is converted into a bolus, and introduced into the stomach?'

'Now you are surely laughing at me.'

'Oh no, I'm not, all that is most true and interesting; but tell me what do you know?'

'Well, sir, I know that I am hungry, and that this is a good dinner.'

This would be the common-sense and appropriate answer. Even the physiologist, when he is hungry, does not think much of *how* he eats. The two great points are, that he is hungry, and that he has a good dinner. Some are hungry and have not the good food, others have the food and are not hungry. But the qualification for enjoying food is not a knowledge of how to eat, but the being hungry. We do not need to know *how* we are born again in order to be saved. We do not need to know all or anything about the Spirit's work within us in order to get peace (there were people, in Acts xix. 2, who were believers and yet who said, "We have not so much as heard whether there be any Holy Ghost"), but we must know about Christ's work *for* us before we can be saved. The greatest physiologist might die of hunger. We might know everything about the Spirit's work and yet be lost for ever, because we had not received and rested upon Christ offered to us in the gospel.

We are justified by *faith*, but the experience of what goes on within us is sensation and not *faith*.

Some men seem to have a difficulty with anxious souls (believing them to be dead), to know what to advise them to do. It is the Spirit that quickeneth. Some, therefore, tell sinners at once to pray for the Spirit, thinking thus to simplify matters by reducing it to reason—as it seems very plain, since the Spirit quickens, nothing is easier than to cry for that Spirit. But it is not so easy, for a dead man cannot cry. Some, again, tell them to believe the record God gave of His Son—to believe in the Lord Jesus Christ. A dead man cannot speak, and of course a dead man cannot believe, so we are in an equal difficulty. Praying and believing are alike impossible with the unregenerate man, without the quickening of the Spirit of God. The great point is to find out what we are commanded to do, what is our duty to do. It is to tell every man the good news, and press him instantly to believe it. It is the

Spirit that is the agent, but He always uses the truth as the instrument, the truth about a crucified and now risen Christ. Faith does not come by feeling, trying, or praying, but by *hearing*. The moment I accept Christ as my own individual personal Saviour who put away my sin, I am warranted to believe that I am born again, and the Spirit in the new man will lust against the flesh in the old man. Peace, indeed, I have with God, Christ Himself being our peace, but I have no peace with myself. 'Being justified by faith' (in contrast to 'by works') 'we have peace with God through our Lord Jesus Christ.' There is a faith that is human, and a faith that is Spirit-wrought. The plan is of God; the redemption, the truth, and the faith are all of God. But how can I know whether I have God-wrought faith? Does my faith take hold of what is going on within? That is not of God. Does my faith take hold of, is it taken up with, what was done eighteen hundred years ago on Calvary, and with Him who suffered there? This is God-honouring and saving faith. This is being born of the Spirit. The Spirit by the truth introduces Christ as the life into my dead soul. This is quickening, *the renewing* of the Holy Ghost. The Holy Ghost thus gives a *new* nature.

II. INDWELT BY THE SPIRIT.

In John iv. 14 we read of the indwelling of the Spirit, 'as a well of water springing up into everlasting life.' This is said only of Christians. The

Spirit of God dwells in [...]
He has quickened, and He [...]
He has quickened (Rom. viii. [...]
greater measure than in others; [...]
have not the Spirit of Christ, he [...]
Therefore, all who are Christ's [...]
dwelling in them. There is a [...]
separating Christ and the Spirit in [...]
in regeneration of *confounding* Chr[...]
us with the Spirit's work in us. I[...]
with Christ, a son as Christ is a s[...]
Christ is, that the Spirit dwells in [...]
even as He dwelt in Christ, of course [...]
out measure.

It is thus we have *access*, for thro[...]
'we have access by one Spirit to the F[...]

It is thus that we can *worship* tha[...]
spirit and in truth. This lesson He [...]
poor confessed sinner at Sychar's well.

It is thus that we are practically [...]
more and more separated from evil, for [...]
'*Holy* Ghost,' the 'Spirit of holiness.'

It is thus we are *comforted and guid*[...]
the Lord Jesus said, If I go away I will [...]
Comforter, (literally *paraclete*, which [...]
much more than comfort). This same [...]
used in 1 John ii. 1, for Christ the A[...]
(literally *paraclete*), one who looks after [...]
interests. And thus, as Christ looks after [...]
interests before God, so the other *Paraclete*
after all Christ's interests as connected w[...]
while we are passing through the wildern[...]

divine Servant leading us into all truth; for here again the truth is His channel. He is our divine friend on earth, for He points us to Christ.

Thus we *live* in the Spirit (all Christians being dead and risen with Christ); and the exhortation is founded on this, 'Let us also *walk* in the Spirit' (Gal. v. 25), principally as being connected with Christ and the members of His body, in every member of which the Spirit dwells. We are to walk in the Spirit, for instance in the practical exercise of brotherly love, and not be *walking as men*. What! are we not *men?* No; we are sons of God indwelt by the Spirit. Men walk in selfishness. The walk in the Spirit is each esteeming another better than himself.

Thus we are '*led* of the Spirit' (Gal. v. 18). All Christians are led. This is not an exhortation, but a privilege. 'For as *many* as are led by the Spirit of God, they are the sons of God,' and all believers are sons. But though in each Christian the Spirit dwells, the exhortation is given, 'Be filled with the Spirit' as with the air you breathe, so live in the presence of glory, in the light, in fellowship with Father and Son, and thus the atmosphere will be 'the Spirit.' He is spoken of as

1. *A witness*. (1 John v. 6.) He bears true witness, He tells the truth concerning Christ, He is a witness to Christ's having come by water and blood; and every Christian has Him dwelling within him, as we also see in Rom. viii., a witness that we are sons. He is the witness of love and accomplished redemption.

2. *A seal.* As goods a[re sealed by the]
purchaser after they become hi[s, so when we]
believe, we are sealed. Only [then.]
The oil was put on the blood of the [cleans-]
ing. (Lev. xiv. 25, 28.) In th[ese days]
many these go together; but many, [as in]
Apostolic days, though they knew the[ir sins]
forgiven, did not know they had et[ernal life. A]
quickened soul is not necessarily an [indwelt]
soul.

3. *An earnest.* He is the earnest of [our inheri-]
tance—that is, part of it that we po[ssess now.]
The Israelites got the grapes from E[shcol, being]
still in the desert. In Rom. viii. 17 [we are]
children (the Spirit bearing witness), a[nd so]
sealed; 'but, if children, then heirs; he[irs of God]
and joint-heirs with Christ.' Therefore, [a man,]
as heir, has not taken the inheritance, w[e do not]
possess it, but suffer now, having the ea[rnest of]
the inheritance, until the redemption of [the pur-]
chased possession. 'Ourselves also who h[ave the]
first-fruits of the Spirit, even we ourselve[s groan]
within ourselves, waiting for the adoption, [to wit,]
the redemption of the body.' (Rom. viii. [23.])

III. COMMUNICATING THE SPIRIT.

In John vii. 38, we read, 'He that believ[eth on]
Me, out of his belly shall flow rivers of l[iving]
water.' Thus those who have been quick[ened]
and who are indwelt by the Spirit, are no[w the]
channels through which He is ministered to ot[hers.]
The waters in the desert flowed from a smitten

The water flowed from Christ's wounded side, and it is only as we are smitten, exercised, subdued, that these rivers will flow from us. Only as we come thus to Christ and drink, shall living waters flow from us. Alas! how little we see of the Spirit flowing from those professing to be quickened by the Spirit. Is it not because we are drawing little from the great fountain-head? 'Let him come unto Me and drink.' It is only through saved sinners that God is now to send forth His river of life. 'The love of God is shed abroad in our hearts by the Holy Ghost.' And this love of God we are to pour out in rivers on this arid desert as witnesses of God; first, by carrying the gospel to our fellow-sinners, and telling of that Christ whom we know, and who is offered to them; and, secondly, by ministering love to all the saints of God in building up and comforting them. And it is only as our own affections and thoughts, that is, all our inner man, is filled with the pure water from the fountain, that the rivers can flow.

In connection with the three operations of the Spirit of God which we have been considering, namely, *the being quickened, being indwelt, and communicating*, we may look—1st. At Christ Himself; 2d. At the Church corporately; 3d. At each individual believer—

1st. As quickened by the Spirit.

Christ was born of the Spirit. This was His incarnation as we read in the angel's answer to Mary in Luke i. 35. 'That holy thing which shall be born of thee shall be called the Son of

God.' (Luke i. 35.) The meat-offering had to be mingled with oil. (Lev. ii. 4.)

The Church corporately in the *resurrection* of Christ (Rom. i. 4; 1 Peter i. 3). He was quickened by the Spirit, as the Head of the body (1 Peter iii. 18).

The *individual* believer; when the Spirit applies the truth to his conscience (James i. 18). 'Of His own will begat He us with the word of truth.'

2d. Indwelt by the Spirit.

Christ we see sealed with the Spirit when, at His baptism, the Spirit as a dove rested on Him. The meat-offering had to be anointed with oil. (Lev. ii. 4.) 'Him hath God the Father sealed.' (John vi. 27.)

The Church, we see at Pentecost not merely quickened but formed into a temple for God on the earth: the true temple, filled with the true glory. And we see this accomplished in fulfilment of Acts i. 8. 'Ye shall receive power after that the Holy Ghost is come upon you, and ye shall be witnesses *unto me*, (1) both in Jerusalem and in all Judea, (2) and in Samaria, (3) and unto the uttermost part of the earth.' The Holy Ghost thus fell on—

1. The Jews, when they were *waiting in prayer* (Acts ii. 4,) in obedience to the resurrection command of our Lord, 'Wait for the promise of the Father which ye have heard of Me.' (Acts i. 4.) They had heard of Him in John xiv. to xvi.

2. The people of Samaria, by the *laying on of the Apostles' hands*. (Acts viii. 17.)

3. The Gentiles in the *preaching of the Word*. (Acts x. 44.) And thus is the Spirit now given. In this latter method was the proper Gentile pentecost our pentecost. Thus it is in the preaching of the Word that we are to expect the blessing of the Spirit.

As regards the *individual*, indwelling is seen in his sealing: when by believing the record he receives his emancipation, his conscious liberty and peace with God, takes his place as a son, with the Holy Ghost as the testifier, and with Him as the earnest waits for the inheritance.

3. Communicating the Spirit.

Christ in His ministry and prophetic work communicated the Spirit.

The Church is seen communicating the Spirit, in the preaching of the apostles, at and subsequent to Pentecost; in the Scriptures they have left; and in all collective testimony down to the present time, that has been in accordance with the Word of God.

Individuals, in the outflow of love in our place in the wilderness, and in ministry, as evangelists, teachers, or pastors, or in any other service to God.

These words, BORN, INDWELT, and COMMUNICATING, have their opposites severally in the three words spoken about the Spirit, RESIST, GRIEVE, and QUENCH.

I. The Spirit may be *resisted*.

Acts vii. 51: 'Ye stiff-necked and uncircumcised in heart and ears, ye do always resist the Holy Ghost.' This is addressed to the unconverted who resist Him as a *quickener*.

II. The Spirit may be *grieved*.

Eph. iv. 30 : 'Grieve not the Holy Spirit of God, whereby ye are sealed unto the day of redemption. This is addressed only to saved people, who can grieve him as an *indwelling* Spirit. This shews what a friend He is to us. If you had committed some great sin, your friend would be grieved, your enemy would be rejoiced. You can grieve only a friend. What a touching appeal, fellow-believer ? What will the consequence be ? In love He will reprove. He will rebuke our consciences, until we are consciously cleansed, and He can again dwell in us ungrieved.

III. The Spirit may be *quenched*.

1 Thess. v. 19 : 'Quench not the Spirit.' Many have been perplexed with this text, thinking that it had reference to the *indwelling* of the Spirit. You may grieve Him thus, but no believer can quench Him thus; 'For they shall never perish ;' but the next verse, 'Despise not prophesying,' explains it. A Christian cannot quench the Spirit in himself, but by refusing to allow Him to work through a fellow Christian, he thus may quench Him. It is thus in His communications that the Spirit may be quenched.

As He can be resisted in His testimony, which is His instrument in *quickening;* and grieved in His person, as *indwelling,* so He can be quenched in His gifts as *communicating.* If I despise the humblest channel that God has formed and filled to dispense His streams of life, and put a sluice upon their flow, I stop His testimony, I quench the Spirit. It has nothing whatever to do with the indwelling of the Spirit. That can never be quenched; for the foundation of God standeth sure. But what a solemn warning in this day of self-seeking and pretensions! *Resist* is the word applied to the unconverted. *Grieve* is that applied to the individual Christian. *Quench* is that which has reference to the saints when gathered together, waiting on the Spirit.

The sin against the Holy Ghost has often been spoken about. All sin is against the Holy Ghost. What Christ spoke about in such solemn and awful words in Matt. xii., was '*blasphemy* against the Holy Ghost;' and if the context is looked at it will be seen that this blasphemy consisted in giving Satan the credit of doing what was known to be God's work.

Bring your ignorance to the Holy Spirit, the great teacher, who by His precious truth will lead you into all truth.

> No, not the love without the blood;
>   That were to me no love at all;
> It could not reach my sinful soul,
>   Nor hush the fears which me appal.
>
> I need the love, I need the blood,
>   I need the grace, the cross, the grave,
> I need the resurrection-power,
>   A soul like mine to purge and save.
>
> The love I need is righteous love,
>   Inscribed on the sin-bearing tree,
> Love that exacts the sinner's debt,
>   Yet, in exacting, sets him free.

Love that condemns the sinner,
  Yet, in condemning, pardons him;
That saves from righteous wrath,
  In saving, righteousness reveals.

Love boundless as Jehovah's self,
  Love holy as His righteous law,
Love unsolicited, unbought,
  The love proclaimed on Golgotha.

This is the love that calms my heart,
  That soothes each conscience-pang within;
That pacifies my guilty dread,
  And frees me from the power of sin.

The love that blotteth out each stain,
  That plucketh hence each deadly sting;
That fills me with the peace of God,
  Unseals my lips and bids me sing.

The love that liberates and saves,
  That this poor straitened soul expands;
That lifts me to the heaven of heavens,
  The shrine above not made with hands.

The love that quickens into zeal,
  That makes me self-denied and true,
That leads me out of what is old,
  And brings me into what is new.

That purifies and cheers and calms,
  That knows no change and no decay;
The love that loves for evermore,
  Celestial sunshine, endless day

'Heaven Opened.'

OUR STUDY.

THE gates have closed that guard the way to the tree of life. The flaming sword turns *every* way, so that no flesh can approach and live. Man has sinned. God is righteous. Well might angels weep as they behold such a sight. HEAVEN IS SHUT. God dwells in His secret place. Thunders and lightnings are round about Him. Clouds of thickest darkness hide Him from man. The blood of Abel's lamb, the rejection of Cain's first-fruits, attest the fact. Heaven is shut. The blood-sprinkled door-posts, the thousands of altars, the myriads of bleeding victims, the smoke ever ascending from the fires of judgment, the unceasing priestly work, all proclaim that heaven's doors are shut.

But *promise* shone through the dark cloud of *judgment*, and the glory of One coming to deliver was revealed; and while the captive Israelite sat in his desolation beside the river of Chebar, he wrote, 'The heavens were opened, and I saw visions of God.' (Ezek. i. 1.) Thus we see heaven opened concerning,

I. CHRIST IN PROPHECY.

And it is God who opens it, it is God who shews the visions. The visions were about the glory of God and His relation to Israel: the cloud, the chariot of His glory then departing as with wings and wheels from His dwelling on earth. His ancient people are seen scattered and broken, but the heavens do not close (in vision) until again the glory of God fills the temple, and the whole earth besides is filled with His glory, and heaven and earth are finally united under the righteous sway of the Prince of Peace, the coming Deliverer. May He hasten that glorious day!

II. CHRIST IN OBEDIENCE.

But turn now to another scene,—Matt. iii. 16. In Jordan's waters stands a spotless, perfect Man, in the place where the godly Jews confessed sin in the baptism of repentance. Grace (not sin) has brought Him hither, that He might fulfil all righteousness; and when He came as the perfect servant, the obedient man, 'Lo, THE HEAVENS WERE OPENED unto Him, and He saw the Spirit of God descending like a dove, and lighting upon Him; and lo, a voice from heaven, saying, This is My beloved Son, in whom I am well pleased.' This is heaven opening on Christ in obedience.

The Lord Jesus Christ was the only perfectly obedient man that earth has seen. Never had earth beheld such a sight, the glorious sun had never before risen on such a day. God is looking down from an opened heaven upon a Man, and on that Man His eye can rest with perfect satisfaction, perfect complacency. God declares Him to be His Son. As Man, He is anointed for His work with the seal of the Father. The Holy Ghost descends on the meek, the lowly, the obedient One. He Himself is the Person on whom the *heavens open*. The Father testifies of Him; the Holy Ghost testifies of Him; the eyes of the believing ones are turned towards Him. On no other object in this God-hating, God-rejecting world, could God's eye have rested. The Spirit, like the dove of Noah, looked over all the waste of waters and found no rest but on the ark. He was the solitary witness for God in this world which He had made: so if the scene is an opened heaven and God looking down upon the earth, the sole attraction there is Jesus, the Son of God, the Son of man.

> 'It is the Father's voice that cries,
> 'Mid the deep silence of the skies,
> This, this is My beloved Son,
> In Him I joy, in Him alone.'

Again, we read of heaven being opened (John i. 51) in connection with

III. CHRIST IN GOVERNMENT.

Here we have an intimation of the future righteous and peaceful government of earth united with heaven under the Son of man—where our

Lord Himself says, 'Verily, verily I say unto you, hereafter ye shall see HEAVEN OPEN, and the angels of God ascending and descending upon the Son of man.' Nathanael, the representative of the godly Jews, had confessed Him to be the Son of God and King of Israel; and our Lord now told him that those who received Him when He was on earth, should see yet greater things than those by which they had been convinced; and further, they should see *heaven open*, and He who had come down to be the *Son of man*, the Man of sorrows, should, in that name, be the object of the ministry of God's highest creatures. This will be true in all its fulness to those of Israel whom Nathanael represented, in a coming day. Meantime, we see heaven open, and all the ministry between heaven and earth carried on through Him. Our thoughts are taken back to Jacob at his 'Bethel' (Gen. xxviii. 12), where, from his pillow of stone, a ladder reached to heaven, on which angels ascended and descended, and we see the Lord Jesus uniting earth to heaven, for He has been raised up and set at His Father's right hand; and in Him we are raised from the grave of earth to the seats in heaven, quickened together with Christ, raised up together, and made to sit together in heavenly places in Him. The scene is changed, but the object to which all eyes are turned is the same. An opened heaven no longer looks upon the Son of God in humiliation, but upon that same Son of man uniting heaven and earth, God and His creature, and on Him as the object of the ministry of the angelic hosts. Blessed time for this poor groaning misgoverned earth! Then shall be known the full power of the Lord of hosts, who has said that He will 'open the windows of heaven, and pour out a blessing, that there shall not be room enough to receive it.' (Mal. iii. 10.) Meantime, we gladly take rejection with Him, until He sits on His own throne, for if we suffer with Him, we shall also reign with Him. Our next spectacle of an open heaven is the sample of what an open heaven sees now on earth, and our place here under the kings of the earth who are plotting against the Lord and His anointed. Heaven is opened on

IV. CHRIST IN THE GLORY OF GOD,

To the rejected disciple. (Acts vii. 55.) 'Stephen, being full of the Holy Ghost, looked up stedfastly into heaven, and saw the glory of God, and Jesus standing on the right hand of God, and said, behold, I see the HEAVENS OPENED, and the Son of man standing on the right hand of God.' Man had rejected Christ; God had taken Him to His own right hand. Man, in his most inveterate hatred of God, had sent out of the world the only Person in it on whom God's eye could gaze with complacency. Heaven can open now upon nothing on this earth. When it opens, it is itself the scene; but the object to the mind of God, and to the believer full of the Holy Ghost, is still the same Jesus. Stephen was being sent after his

Master. The Third Person of the Trinity in H[is]
was being rejected as the Second Person had b[een]
at the cross. The Son of man would still st[and]
ready to return, until this testimony had be[en]
rejected; He is now *set down*, waiting till [His]
enemies are made His footstool. What a glori[ous]
sight to the believer in testimony, in rejection,
martyrdom! He sees not the enraged multitu[de,]
he hears not the derisive shout, he beholds [not]
the fiendish gesture, 'he sees *heaven opened.*'
seems as if, even during the time that they w[ere]
stoning him, he kept his eyes fixed on this w[on-]
derful vision, for we read at verse 59, ' and th[ey]
stoned Stephen calling upon God, and sayi[ng,]
Lord Jesus, receive my spirit.'

So it is with us now. Heaven opened *on* [the]
Lord Jesus; it opens *to* us. Whatever enmity [of]
men or devils may be around us, faith now s[ees]
heaven opened and the Son of man at the ri[ght]
hand of God for us. It is no longer the eye of G[od]
delighting to look through an opened heaven up[on]
His Son on earth, it is the Christian himself loo[k-]
ing from earth into an opened heaven, a[nd]
seeing all the glory of God, and better than [all]
the glory, and, above the highest of even Go[d's]
heavenly glories, 'the Son of man,' there for hi[m.]

Never before had such a sight been seen,
glorified MAN at God's right hand. Prophets h[ad]
spoken of it—but here was the fact. Glory w[as]
native to heaven—but now we see the *Son* [of]
man in the glory of God. What a gospel f[or]
every sinner, for every son of man, did Steph[en]

preach, when, filled with the Spirit, he told out that heaven was opened, and the Son of man was there! Is my reader a weak and trembling one, who can hardly dare to think that he is saved, and quite conscious that he has never been filled with the Holy Ghost? Listen to the glorious good news that God Himself has commanded to be told to every one: *heaven is opened*—the veil is rent—God's hand has done it; not open now merely for God to look on us, but open for us to look upon God. The gates of Eden have been opened—Christ is the Door—and further, He as *Son of man* is there. As Son of God He never required to leave that glory and go back to it again; but as Son of man He never would have been there unless God had been vindicated —had been glorified in the putting away of sin —sin that lay upon Him as the substitute of the sinner. 'It is finished.' This is God's good news; a quickened sinner, an open heaven, and an exalted Substitute! This is the ground of my peace. Not what I *feel*, not the suppression of God-dishonouring thoughts, not success in the conflict, not growth in grace, not the feeling of an indwelling Spirit, not a growing more like God, but the sure testimony of God to an open heaven and the Son of man before Him. What more do we need than what God has done?

The tombs are rent as if to show that the sinner is to meet God now in life, in resurrection; therefore Stephen, a poor sinner, stands filled with the Holy Ghost.

The veil is rent to show that the way into the holiest of all is now made manifest, therefore heaven is open to the believing sinner.

The Lord is risen, and is at the right hand of God, and He is there the Son of man for me. An unveiled God, an open tomb, a glorified Son of man—what more, guilty, trembling soul, do you want? The natural eye has never seen this; *faith* alone, by the Holy Ghost, beholds such a glory. Light from earth has never pierced the midnight darkness in which God is enveloped. The flaming sword still turns every way to guard 'the tree of life,' but where it fell. It fell on Christ, and in Him the sword of vengeance will never be turned against us. There is no entrance into Paradise but by the Door. There is no mercy to sinners but in Christ. The world knew not the darkness in which God wrapped His Son, when on the cross He was dealing with sin. The last hour of light the world had men spent in wagging their heads at, and spitting upon, the Light of Life. No unquickened man saw Christ in resurrection. (Acts x. 41.) Faith alone can see Him thus. The self-emptied sinner alone can rest, where God has found rest, in the glorified Son of man.

Once again we see heaven opened. In Acts x. 11, Peter '*saw heaven opened*, and a certain vessel descending unto him as it had been a great sheet, knit at the four corners, and let down to the earth.' Heaven is opened to explain the mystery of

5. THE CHURCH FORMED.

The Church of God had been hid in God. It is not according to earthly and Jewish distinctions of clean and unclean. It is not according to the thought that the Moabite and Ammonite should not come into the Israelitish congregation of God. This was true (Neh. xiii. 1)—is true and ever will be true. But, here is something new. The middle wall of partition is broken down, and there is neither Jew nor Gentile. This was never revealed or prophesied about before. The Gentile was to be blessed, but mediately through the Jew; and that will yet take place. Peter saw clean and unclean on an equality, not the unclean benefited by the clean. Those that were nigh, and those that were far off, that is, the Jews nationally separated to God, and the Gentiles outside God's calling, all now stand equally guilty, and equally to be blessed by God. To Peter had been given the Keys of the Kingdom (not of the Church), and he opened the doors first to the Jews in his sermon in Acts ii. at Pentecost; and then, after this heaven-given vision, to the Gentiles, in the person of the centurion (Acts x. 44); and since the door has thus been opened equally to both, no national distinction being recognised, this key is no longer necessary. We now have the Holy Ghost sent down from heaven. This is the vision of the true dwelling-place of God on the earth— the body of Christ. The middle wall of partition between Jew and Gentile was broken down, and

106

His servants were sent to
nation, kindred, and tongue
is to consist of all kinds of
the ages to come 'He might
riches of His grace.' May we
on Christ, and thus doing His
His work of ingathering now,
Him in the glory above! For
heaven opened on

6. THE CHURCH SEATED

'After this, I looked, and behold
opened in heaven. And the first
heard . . . said, Come up hither, and
thee things which must be hereafter.'
&c.) In the apocalyptic vision, John
the Son of man in glory, as the first
great divisions of the vision. (Rev. i.
also seen God's Church history—'the
are '—the second great division in the
the seven Churches. (Rev. ii., iii.) And
to behold 'the things which must be
as the third division. But the Church
in the throned elders has been caught up
iv.), and is now seen seated with
thrones (Rev. iv.) before all the judgment
out. The Saints shall judge the world
are like Abraham, the friend of God, a
Sodom, hearing all that is to fall on Sodom
is what we are waiting for, to be caught
meet the Lord in the air, and to be set
on His throne. (Rev. iii. 21.) What a

'Heaven Opened.'

[th]e martyred Stephen! This is the Church [trium]phant, that was the Church militant. Well [may] we praise the Lord for this little glimpse [of an] opened heaven, for He would have our [heart]s to rest on the blessed thought that we shall [be en]throned around the crowned Jesus, before [He c]omes to execute His wrath. For this is not [all.] Again heaven will be opened, not in the [visio]n of prophecy, not on the meek lowly Jesus, [nor] on His suffering people, nor to show His [heavenl]y seated Church, but to show

7. CHRIST AND HIS SAINTS IN JUDGMENT.

[H]e comes with myriads of His saints. Christ [and] the Church is now seen rising up in the [exer]cise of judgment, as John says in Rev. xix. [:—] 'I saw HEAVEN OPENED, and behold a white [hors]e; and He that sat upon Him was called [Fait]hful and True, and in righteousness He doth [judg]e and make war. His eyes were as a flame [of fi]re, and on His head were many crowns: and [He] had a name written, that no man knew but [He] Himself. And He was clothed with a vesture [dipp]ed in blood: and His name is called The [WO]RD OF GOD (John i. 1). And the armies in [hea]ven followed Him upon white horses, clothed [in fi]ne linen, white and clean. And out of His [mou]th goeth a sharp sword, that with it He [sho]uld smite the nations: and He shall rule [the]m with a rod of iron; and He treadeth the [win]e-press of the fierceness and wrath of Almighty [Go]d. *And He hath* on His vesture and on His thigh a name written KING OF KINGS, AND LORD OF LORDS.' Such is the awful opening of heaven upon a God-dishonouring earth when the rejected, crucified Son of man shall disperse the midnight darkness in which the earth is wrapped, by the flash of His judgment-sword. That funeral pall of blackest die which has hung over this doomed world from the sixth hour of that most awful crucifixion day, shall be torn asunder by His hand when He executes judgment. Then will be seen, not the deluge of water, as when in Gen. vii. 11, the windows of heaven were opened, but wrath from heaven, the wrath of the Lamb. What a day! what a reality! The book of mercy closed! Christ risen up! The door shut! The sword unsheathed! How the scene is changed! No longer humiliation; no longer angelic ministry, no longer His martyred followers; but His fierce vengeance, His own right hand, His own sword girt on His thigh, His now triumphant co-heirs riding forth in victory and breaking to pieces all before Him. Still the object is Jesus, the WORD of God. For it is Christ Himself who is our study, let Him be on earth, in heaven, or joining earth to heaven, rejected or reigning, suffering or subduing. That same pierced brow which wore the thorny crown is now to be decked with many crowns, for,

> 'The crowns that are now round the false one's brow
> Shall be worn by earth's rightful Lord.'

That same pierced hand shall draw the sword from

its scabbard; those same wounded feet shall press the snowy clouds, and 'every eye shall see Him, and they also that pierced Him: and all kindreds of the earth shall wail because of Him.' God Himself breaks the silence; everything is now felt by every one to be REAL. The oft-rejected Christ is seen to be real; the scorned judgment is seen to be real; an open heaven is seen to be real; an eternal hell is seen to be real; the winepress of the fierceness and wrath of Almighty God is seen to be real; the wrath of the Lamb is seen to be real.

Flee from the wrath to come, and study Christ, who has opened heaven, and who is all the glory within an opened heaven.

> Heaven was opened—Jesus came;
> He revealed the Father's name,
>   Took our place to bear our load,
> God has owned Him from above,
> Sent the Spirit like a dove,
>   Sealed Him, and with Him abode.—MATT. iii. 16.
>
> Heaven is opened—Lo! we see
> Christ who died upon the tree
>   Joining earth to heaven above—JOHN i. 51.
> Angels servants from the throne
> Blessings bring through Him alone:
>   Richest tokens of His love.
>
> Heaven is opened—glorious day,
> Christ hath put our sin away;
>   Men of every tongue and race,
> Jew and Gentile, bond and free,
> All are welcome equally,—ACTS x. 11.
>   All may share God's matchless grace.

Heaven is opened—Christ has gone
Into heaven, His work is done;
    Him we follow, Him alone.
He whom men have crucified,
Son of man now glorified,—Acts vii. 55.
    Sits upon His Father's throne.

Heaven is opened—on the throne
See the One whom men disown—Rev. iv., xi.
    Now the judge of quick and dead.
Lo! the temple, Christ the light,
He who by His wondrous might
    Bruised for ever Satan's head.

Heaven will open yet again,—Rev. xix. 11.
We with Him shall judge and reign.
    Every eye shall see His face,
Proud rebellious men shall quail,
Nations, kindreds, all shall wail,
    All who scorned His truth and grace.

Triumph and Conflict

OUR STATE.

'AS SORROWFUL, YET ALWAYS REJOICING' —Such was Paul's experience. (2 Cor. vi. 10.) The saved man is a great mystery to the unsaved; happy, yet sad; triumphing, yet troubled; having no sin on him, and yet having sin in him; having no condemnation, and still having fearful conflict. Saved now, yet working out his salvation and waiting for salvation. Even among saved men themselves there is great misunderstanding. Some are engaged more with the triumph side, others with the conflict side of a Christian's experience. We find both most fully brought out in Scripture, each having its own place and importance. The Christian's conflict takes rise and character from his triumph. We get much instruction by looking at the illustrations of a believer's triumph, walk and conflict, as contained in the figures of the Old Testament; for we know that 'Whatsoever things were written aforetime were written for our learning, that we through patience and comfort of the Scriptures might have hope.' (Rom. xv. 4.) Let us look at Israel's history. We find the Israelites

1. Sheltered by blood from God's hand in judg-

ment in Egypt, and testifying for God in the midst of godlessness.

2. Redeemed by power. Taken through the Red Sea by the power of God's might, and living by faith in the wilderness.

3. Entered into their possessions, and in Canaan fighting the battles of the Lord. Let us look at these in detail.

I.—SHELTERED BY BLOOD.

THE ISRAELITE IN EGYPT.

'The Lord spake unto Moses and Aaron in the land of Egypt, saying, This month shall be unto you the beginning of months: it shall be the first month of the year to you. Speak ye unto all the congregation of Israel, saying, In the tenth day of this month they shall take to them every man a lamb. . . . Your lamb shall be without blemish, a male of the first year. . . . And they shall take of the blood and strike it on the two side posts and on the upper door post of the houses wherein they shall eat it. . . . For I will pass through the land of Egypt this night, and will smite all the first-born in the land of Egypt, both man and beast, and against all the gods of Egypt I will execute judgment: I am Jehovah. And the blood shall be to you for a token upon the houses where you are, and *when I see the blood I will pass over you*, and the plague shall not be upon you, to destroy you, when I smite the land of Egypt.' (Exodus xii.) In Egypt the Israelite had thus a triumph and also a conflict.

1. *Triumph.*—He rejoiced because he trusted to the blood on the lintel, and to the word of his Jehovah God, who had said, 'When I see the blood I will pass over you.' So the Christian in this world rejoices, not in the thought that he is pure and sinless, but in the fact that Christ died for his sins. We see this fully explained in the Epistle to Romans (iii. 21 to v. 11).

- God could pass over because the blood was on the lintel.

Thus God can now justify the ungodly.

'When I see the blood I will pass over you.' (Exod. xii. 13.)   'Being now justified by His blood.' (Rom. v. 9.)

The Israelite could rejoice, because he believed God.

The believer can rejoice, being at peace with God.

'The blood shall be to you for a token.' (Exod. xii. 13.)   'Being justified by faith we have peace with God.' (Rom. v. 1.)

Sheltered by blood, we feast upon the roasted Lamb with bitter herbs, unleavened bread, and in the pilgrim garb—at perfect peace, for 'it is Christ that died.'

> Heirs of salvation,
>   Chosen of God;
> Past condemnation,
>   Sheltered by blood.
> Even in Egypt feed we on the Lamb,
> Keeping the statutes of God the I AM.

> In the world around 'tis night,
> Where the feast is spread 'tis bright,
> Israel's Lord is Israel's light.
> 'Tis Jesus, 'tis Jesus, our Saviour from above,
> 'Tis Jesus, 'tis Jesus, 'tis Jesus whom we love.

2. *Conflict.*—There would have been *an unscriptural conflict* in Egypt, if an Israelite had tried by any and every means to put off the hand that was crying for blood, except by God's own ordained means, the blood on the lintel; the acceptance of God's estimate of the value of the blood that He Himself had appointed. This unscriptural conflict we find in modern times, in man's effort by prayers and religiousness, and penances, and sorrows, to live a good *life,* when God is demanding the *death* of the sinner for his sins. And how often do we see the sad spectacle of a man in a condemned world trying to get up religion or devotion, or something else to meet the wrath of God against his sins, when he is condemned already! This is the state of man as depicted in Rom: i. 18, to iii. 20.

But there is a *scriptural conflict*—namely, the conflict against

THE WORLD.

The Christian presents a strange anomaly that cannot be seen perfectly in the figure of an Israelite sheltered by blood in Egypt. He has been taken entirely out of Egypt, and yet he is sent back to Egypt, as the Lord Jesus said to His Father in John xvii. 18, concerning His followers,

'As thou hast sent Me into the world, even so have I also sent them into the world.' According to the illustration, every Christian in one aspect, and a very practical aspect, is still in Egypt, that is the world 'which spiritually is called Egypt where also our Lord was crucified.' (Rev. xi. 8). So our Lord Jesus prayed:—'I pray not that thou shouldest take them out of the world, but that thou shouldest keep them from the evil.' (John xvii. 15.) Being thus in the world and not of it, with souls saved, but with bodies still liable to disease and death, and all creation being under the curse, 'We that are in this tabernacle do groan being burdened, not for that we would be unclothed but clothed upon, that mortality might be swallowed up of life.' (2 Cor. v. 4.) And 'we know that the whole creation groaneth and travaileth in pain together until now. And not only they, but ourselves also which have the first fruits of the Spirit, even we ourselves groan within ourselves waiting for the adoption, to wit, the redemption of our body.' (Rom. viii. 23.) These are groans which should not be stifled, but encouraged. The more that we are in harmony with the mind of God the more will these groanings be heard; not the groanings of an anxious soul to get peace which God has already provided and presented, but the groanings of the saint who is waiting for his body to be fashioned like unto Christ's body of glory. This is evidently quite different from fighting against indwelling corruption. We are waiting like the Israelites till all the chosen of the Lord shall have the blood on the lintel, which will be completed only when the Lord comes. We have been sent into this world to persuade men to come under the protecting power of the blood of Christ, and thus be sheltered from wrath. Meanwhile our place is described in the 17th chapter of John, where we find that the Christian is

Given to Christ out of the world (ver. 6).
Left in the world (vers. 11 and 15).
Not of the world (ver. 14.)
Hated by the world (ver. 14).
Kept from the evil of the world (ver. 15).
Sent into the world (ver. 18.)
Preaching the word to the world (ver. 20).

'God forbid that I should glory save in the cross of our Lord Jesus Christ, by whom the world is crucified unto me and I unto the world.' (Gal. vi. 14.)

II.—REDEEMED BY POWER.

THE ISRAELITES IN THE WILDERNESS.

1. *Triumph.*—A quickened soul is first exercised about what *he has done,*—that he has sinned; and then, as we have seen, he gets peace, because forgiven through the blood of Christ who died for him. But he very soon finds out a further distress, not arising from what he has done, but from what *he is*—*a sinner.* This is described in Rom. v. 12, 'As by one man sin entered into the world.' He has been sheltered from God's hand in judgment,

but he finds he requires a new life in which to serve God. The Israelites found themselves after having been delivered from the death of their firstborn, with *rocks* at either side, *foes* behind, and *the sea* before. So the Christian was *born* a sinner; his own sinful *nature* is unchanged and unchangeable; and the *law* of God is against him—three obstacles much more terrible than those of the Israelites. Many a quickened soul in such a case is ready to cry, 'Hast thou taken us away to die in the wilderness?' (Exod. xiv. 11); 'Who shall deliver me?' (Rom. vii. 24.)

But God does not say, 'I have taken you away to die,' but He says, '*Go forward.*' (Exod. xiv. 15.) God is for us, and His power is exercised through death, through the territory, the last domain of law. Man's extremity is God's opportunity. A way is made in the sea. 'The Lord saved Israel that day out of the hands of the Egyptians: and Israel saw the Egyptians dead upon the sea-shore.' (Exod. xiv. 30). Christ 'was delivered for our offences and raised again for our justification;' 'For if when we were enemies we were reconciled to God by *the death* of His Son, much more being reconciled we shall be saved by *His life*' that is His life in resurrection. Not only are we out of the *house* of bondage, but we are out of the *land* of Egypt. Every Christian has a right to say—'Not only has God sheltered me by blood, but He has saved my soul by His power; not only have I peace with God, but God is for me; not only has God's hand been stayed from visiting me for my sins in wrath, but God's hand has been manifested in destroying all my enemies; not only am I not condemned, but there is no condemnation, not only did Christ die for me, but my standing is in Christ risen from the dead.' (Rom. viii. 1.) Everything as to atonement was completed at Calvary as His own precious dying words assure us, 'It is finished:' His resurrection is the divine proof that it was so. 'It is Christ that died, yea, rather, that is risen again.' (Rom. viii. 34.)

> Pilgrims and strangers,
>   Captives no more;
> Wilderness rangers,
>   Sing we on shore.
> God in His power parted hath the sea,
> Foes all have perished, His people are free.
>   By the pillar safely led,
>   By the manna daily fed,
>   Now the homeward way we tread.
> 'Tis Jesus, 'tis Jesus, our Shepherd here below;
> 'Tis Jesus, 'tis Jesus, 'tis Jesus whom we know.

2. *Conflict.*—There is an *unscriptural Conflict* here also:—How am I as a sinner in the world, under law, to get out of my old standing in Adam and to get into the wilderness with God?

If the Israelites had tried to scale the rocky precipices on either hand, the barriers of nature, instead of taking God's way by a new and supernatural path altogether, it would be an illustration of a quickened sinner trying to climb this mighty obstacle 'born in sin,' this mountain of his nature, instead of taking God's way out of it, as seen in

Romans v. 19, 'As by one man's disobedience many were made sinners, so by the obedience *of One* shall many be made righteous.'

If the Israelites had turned on the foes behind, and had tried to fight their way through, instead of standing still to see the salvation of God, it would be an illustration of a quickened sinner trying to fight against and extirpate his evil nature, or to make it better, and seeking thus to get delivered from the wages of sin, instead of taking God's way in Romans vi. 23, 'eternal life through *Jesus Christ* our Lord.'

If a quickened sinner were to attempt to get deliverance from the power of the law of God and its righteous demands, by trying to make that which cannot be made subject to the law of God a willing servant, he would be like the Egyptians trying to get through where faith alone could walk, 'which the Egyptians assaying to do were *drowned*.' That is the doom of man's efforts; but in Christ Jesus we have died, we have risen. RECKON therefore yourself dead indeed unto sin. It is not that we feel dead to it, or are dead to its motions; but as Christ died to it, so we reckon ourselves dead. If we had no sin in us or *felt* dead to the motions of sin, we could not be told to *reckon* ourselves dead. Instead, however, of crying when I find such a holy law inoperative in bringing my God-hating nature into subjection, 'Who shall deliver me?' (Romans vii. 24), and stopping there, I look back on all my foes dead on the shore. Christ's grave is empty now, and God looks at me as in Christ Jesus. Christ was nailed to Calvary's cross for me, for my sins. Faith in its associating power says, 'I was crucified with Christ.' Faith rests on this fact, that Christ is risen. Faith accepts God's meaning which He has attached to this fact, that I am now not in my sins. I can now sing, in spirit, the triumph song of Moses on the wilderness shore of the Red Sea, and truly say, in the language of Romans viii., 'There is therefore now no condemnation to me in Christ Jesus, for the law of the Spirit of life in Christ Jesus hath made me free from the law of sin and death.'

But also a *scriptural conflict* now begins—namely, the conflict against

THE FLESH.

This is not a conflict to obtain peace nor a conflict to get deliverance from condemnation, nor even that sympathetic and God-honouring groaning of Romans viii. 18-28; but conflict against myself. It is not the conflict against the world. If we look at Israel as an illustration, we find that there were no Egyptians in the wilderness; only Jehovah's congregation was there. We are now shut in with God: God's enemies are our enemies; we are on His side, even against ourselves. We have been crucified and raised; we have sung the song of victory; we triumph in Christ Jesus, and now we have conflict in earnest with our own evil natures. The man who realises that he has got once and for ever into the standing described in Rom. viii. 1, 'There is therefore now no condemnation to them that are in Christ Jesus,' with all his triumph, realises tremendous deadly conflict, not around him, but within him; not struggling to get acceptance with God, but keeping his body under, looking at his own unchanged and unchangeably evil nature within him with something of the abhorrence of God; every day confessing his sin, every day requiring the Advocate. After the Israelites had sung the triumph song on the wilderness shore of the Red Sea, after they had received the pillar cloud to guide them, bread from heaven to feed them, and the water from the rock to refresh them, '*then* came Amalek and fought with Israel in Rephidim.' Does this not give us an illustration of the lusting between the flesh and the Spirit as seen in Galatians v. 17, 'The flesh lusteth against the Spirit, and the Spirit against the flesh, and these are contrary the one to the other?' This 'lusting' or warfare goes on, not that we may cry, 'O wretched man, who shall deliver,' but 'in order that ye may not do the things that ye would.' This is a tremendous personal reality in every saved man. At the same moment that he is rejoicing in Christ Jesus, he has no confidence in the flesh which is still actually within him, and thus he has a warfare every day against himself.

Read Exodus xvii. 8-16, where we get the account of the conflict: Joshua, the captain of the Lord, fights with Amalek, (son of Eliphaz, eldest son of Esau); Moses is on the hill-top with the rod, holding up his hands in intercession to God, supported by Aaron and Hur on either side, for as long as his arms were held up Israel prevailed. And Joshua discomfited Amalek with the edge of the sword. An altar is raised, called 'Jehovah my Banner,' for the Lord will have war with Amalek, not once for all, but *from generation to generation*. This is all after the Red Sea has been crossed.

This gives us an illustration of how the Spirit of Christ fights against the flesh. The Advocate is with the Father on high, and He is 'Jesus Christ the righteous,' the spotless High Priest, making continual intercession for us. The Spirit overcomes the flesh by the word of God. This is all after we have joyfully sung the victory-anthem recorded in Romans viii., 'There is no condemnation to them that are in Christ Jesus.' And indeed we have a specimen of the mighty sword we are now to wield by the Spirit in us, in the practical exhortations laid down in the last chapters of the epistle to the Romans, commencing with chapter xii.

As the Israelites found that the sword of Joshua and the prayers of Moses routed the heathen Amalek, so the Christian finds that there is nothing like the truth of God, the authority of God, the sword of the Spirit, accompanied by the intercession of Christ on high, for the unsubject flesh within him. All the wilderness conflict has this character: 'Thou shalt remember all the way which the Lord thy God led thee these forty years in the wilderness, to *humble* thee and *prove* thee, to *know* what was in thine heart, whether thou wouldst *keep* His commandments or not.' (Deut. viii. 2.)

Brethren in Christ, 'seeing then that ye are risen with Christ, mortify therefore your members which are upon the earth.'

We have triumph because we are forgiven. We have conflict because we are prone to sin.

We have triumph because we are saved. We have conflict because although saved we are but sinners still.

We have triumph over our Adam-nature, for we are not in Adam, but in Christ. We have conflict within us, for, alas! we often 'walk as men.'

We 'are not in the flesh,' therefore we have triumph. The flesh is in us, therefore we have conflict.

We are 'not under law,' therefore we have triumph. The Lord Jesus said, 'If ye love me keep my commandments,' therefore we have conflict. We are not (ὑπο νομον) *under law* neither are we (ανομοι) *lawless*, but we are (εννομοι) *inlawed*— that is *under authority*, or duly subject to Christ.

Christ has taken charge, not only of our salvation, but of our conflict and our walk. Grace saves, but grace also teaches. Neither is it by an internal power only that we are guided, but by external authority or commandment. We do not walk in the paths of righteousness, merely because *we see* them to be righteous, but because God has *ordered* them. The former would be self-pleasing, the latter is God-pleasing; and if ever the question should arise between what I feel and see to be right, and what God says is right, then I must obey God rather than my own feelings. Abraham did not understand how it was right to sacrifice his son, but he believed God, and offered his son because God told him.

As long as the Israelites were in the wilderness, they were seen in themselves as needy and sinful, while God was proving Himself bountiful and gracious. We find a wonderful illustration of God's provision for the Christian's need very near the end of the Israelites' march. In Numbers xxi. we have a sad picture of their murmurings, and at verse 6, we read 'The Lord sent fiery serpents among the people, and they bit the people; and much people of Israel died. Therefore the people came to Moses, and said, We have sinned for we have spoken against the Lord, and against thee; pray unto the Lord, that He take away the serpents from us. And Moses prayed for the people. And the Lord said unto Moses, Make thee a fiery serpent, and set it upon a pole; and it shall come to pass, that every one that is bitten, when he looketh upon it, shall live. And Moses made a serpent of brass, and put it upon a pole, and it came to pass, that if a serpent had bitten any man, when he beheld the serpent of brass, he lived.'

As long as the Christian is in the world, he will have sin in him, and his power against it is

Christ crucified. The Son of Man lifted up on the cross is what withers up practically and daily our rebellion, waywardness and perversity; and in Him God sees no iniquity in Jacob and no perverseness in Israel. And if we say we have no sin, we deceive ourselves, and the truth is not in us.

III.—SEATED IN HEAVENLY PLACES IN CHRIST JESUS.

THE ISRAELITES IN CANAAN.

1. *Triumph.*—Israel under Joshua got through the Jordan, as Israel under Moses got through the Red Sea. If we turn to Joshua iii. 14 to 17 we shall there see the priestly ministry in the passage of Jordan. All Canaan was theirs, 'From the wilderness and this Lebanon even unto the great river, the river Euphrates, all the land of the Hittites, and unto the great sea, toward the going down of the sun, shall be your coast.' (Joshua i. 4.) This was the land flowing with milk and honey; the land in which they were to have long life and prosperity; the land wherein they were to dwell and be fed. The Israelites were blessed with all temporal blessings in earthly places in Canaan. Of us, as Christians, now it is said: God '*hath* blessed us with *all* spiritual blessings in heavenly places in Christ.' Certainly, we have many blessings which we never think of, and never have thought of, but we can think of

none which we do not have in Christ. Every Christian has Christ—nothing less. He may not know all: who does? We strive that we may know Him, that we may grow in grace, and in 'the knowledge of our Lord and Saviour.' In Christ every Christian is blessed with every spiritual blessing in heavenly places.

He is quickened, raised, seated already in heavenly places in Christ. Therefore, according to the illustration, he is in Canaan as to his triumph; for as Christ is, so are we in this world. He is dead, risen, seated, so are we in Him. (Eph. i., ii., iii.)

> Canaan possessors,
>   Safe in the land,
> Victors, confessors;
>   Banner in hand.
> Jordan's deep river evermore behind,
> Cares of the desert no longer in mind.
>   Egypt's stigma rolled away,
>   Canaan's corn our strength and stay,
>   Triumph we the live-long day.
> 'Tis Jesus, 'tis Jesus, the Christ of God alone;
> 'Tis Jesus, 'tis Jesus, 'tis Jesus whom we own.

2. *Conflict.*—There is an *unscriptural conflict* here, as we have seen in Egypt and the wilderness. This conflict is said to be (Eph. vi. 12) 'Not against flesh and blood.' There is more in this simple statement than might at first appear. We are in the world; we are not of it. Our work is not to fight to put the world right. This is the mistake of all who have taken, or may take, the sword to fight the Lord's battles in this dispensa-

tion. We are here to act in grace as children of the Father, and to save men from the world. Our enemies are spiritual, not men in the flesh. We are not sanctified Jews, praying the 109th Psalm, and slaying men, women, and children. That was the right thing in Canaan; it is the wrong thing in the position in which *we* stand, and that, not only when it leads to bloodshed, but wrong in principle, for the principle embraces every wrestling with the weapons of this world. Have I been cheated? what is my remedy? Go to law? Nay. But then I shall suffer loss. Very well, suffer (1 Cor. vi. 7; 1 Pet. ii. 20). The believer is done with all 'flesh and blood' conflict. He may be called a fool, a madman; one that has no interest as a citizen, as a politician, a person of utopian ideas and transcendental schemes. He is content so to be styled, and moreover, he is not to retort. His life is hid with Christ in God. All contact with the world's ways can but defile him. 'Flesh and blood' is not the platform on which he wars. World philanthropists he may admire; world reformers he may be thankful for; but he hears his Master say, 'Let the dead bury their dead' (if decently buried, so much the more agreeable for us), 'follow thou Me.' But there is a *scriptural conflict*, namely, the conflict against

THE DEVIL.

All Canaan was given to Joshua; but we read that they had to enter in and take possession of it personally—'every place that the *sole of your foot shall tread upon*, that have I given unto you.' (Joshua i. 3.) They had to fight for every inch of the land. First Jericho fell, then Ai, until Joshua routed the thirty-one kings. Read Joshua xii. And after we are told that we are already raised and seated in Christ, that we already have been blessed with all spiritual blessings in heavenly places in Christ, the conflict is put before us in the very heavenly places where we are blessed, as Joshua's fighting with Canaan's kings was in Canaan.

This conflict is not against the world or the flesh—we have considered these already—but it is against Satan the accuser, wicked spirits ruling the darkness, demons that hate the light. (Eph. vi. 12.)

1st. What are they? 'Principalities and powers.' They possess strength of evil, strong wills more powerful than ours. They originally derived strength from God, and their apostate will rises from themselves.

2d. What do they do? They have *power* over the world as governing it; for it is in darkness, and they are 'the rulers of the darkness of this world.'

3d. Where do they dwell? They *dwell* 'in heavenly places,' and thus ever endeavour to obtain a religious and delusive ascendancy over us, for they are 'spiritual wickednesses.' And what do we require for these foes who dispute our possessions? This is not Pharaoh keeping us in bondage; nor Amalek fighting against us, but the Canaanites disputing our own possessions. The two former we were saved from; the latter we have to meet in their true attitude, as keeping us from our rightful places as the redeemed of God. We fight, clad in the armour of God. 'Be strong in the Lord, and in the power of His might. Put on the whole armour of God, that ye may be able to stand against the wiles of *the devil*. For we wrestle not against flesh and blood, but against principalities, against powers, against the rulers of the darkness of this world, against spiritual wickedness in heavenly places. Wherefore take unto you the whole armour of God, that ye may be able to withstand in the evil day, and having done all to stand. Stand therefore, having your loins girt about with truth, and having on the breastplate of righteousness; and your feet shod with the preparation of the gospel of peace; above all, taking the shield of faith, wherewith ye shall be able to quench all the fiery darts of the wicked. And take the helmet of salvation, and the sword of the Spirit, which is the word of God: praying always with all prayer and supplication in the Spirit, and watching thereunto with all perseverance and supplication for all saints.' (Eph. vi. 10-18).

This is neither to 'get peace,' nor to avoid condemnation, nor to get into 'heavenly places.' It is not with the judgment of God, nor the law of God, nor sin within me. This conflict is against the wiles of the adversary, who, day and night, tries to deprive me of all that God has given, and all that faith enjoys.

Let us see how all this bears upon us. Some look upon a Christian as out of Egypt, now in the Wilderness, and waiting to reach Canaan. This may have some truth in it, but it does not convey the whole truth as to our position.

Others look upon it thus:—We are in Canaan by faith: we are in the Wilderness in fact; and we may be in Egypt, Wilderness, or Canaan as to experience. Again, there is truth here, but I do not think it is exactly put as Scripture warrants. Let us shortly sum up all the above:—

HEB. xi. 28-30.

I.—'Through faith he (Moses) kept the passover, and the sprinkling of blood, lest he that destroyed the first-born should touch them.'
Exod. xii.—Rom. v. 1-11. Triumph by blood.
John xvii.—Rom. viii. 22-28. Conflict with the WORLD.

II.—'By faith they passed through the Red Sea as by dry land, which the Egyptians assaying to do were drowned.'
Exod. xiv. 15.; xv.—Rom. viii. Triumph in power.
Exod. xvii. 8-16—Gal. v. 17. Conflict with the FLESH.

III.—'By faith the walls of Jericho fell down after they were compassed about seven days.'
Josh. i.—Eph. i.—Triumph in our inheritance.
Josh. xii.—Eph. v.—Conflict with the DEVIL.

'All these things happened unto them for types, and they are written for our admonition' (1 Cor. x. 11). By *faith*, therefore, according to the above parallel, we are *in Christ*, who is far above all Egyptian judgment, all Wilderness weariness, and even all Canaan conflicts. In actual *fact* we are still in the world; and in individual *experience* we have still clouds and sunshine, joy and sorrow, storm and calm. Thus there are three things the Christian has to distinguish: 1st, his Standing; 2nd, his State; 3rd, his Experience,—His standing before God, his state in this world, and his own experience as he passes through this world.

1. THE CHRISTIAN'S STANDING.

All Christians are by faith in the eternal calm of God, having everything that the work of Christ has secured. We are far above all principalities and powers in Him who is alive for evermore, who is the Living One, and was once dead. We are as near to God as Christ is, for we are made nigh by His blood; and we are as dear to God as Christ is, for Our Lord, speaking to His Father, says, 'Thou hast loved them as Thou hast loved Me.' (John xvii. 23) In Him we possess all the fulness of God. But as to fact, we find another side of the truth, which is—

2. THE CHRISTIAN'S STATE.

According as we look at it, all Christians are still in *Egypt*. Not an enemy is really destroyed. The *world* is around us and against us. We are sheltered by blood, and still we are in a condemned world. We are eternally justified, and by grace we are saved persons; still, in plain English, in Scripture language, we are just where we were as to our surroundings.

Again we are, as to fact, still in the *Wilderness*, requiring guidance by the eye of our Father every day. As the Israelites of old had no sign-posts or highways in the trackless desert, and were guided by the pillar-cloud, so human wisdom and human advice can never direct the Christian in his heavenward journey. God's word is His light. As the Israelites had to get their bread daily from heaven, marching through a barren wilderness, so the Christian gets no food for his new nature in that which his fellow-men all around him enjoy. He says, 'The life which I now live in the flesh, I live by the faith of the Son of God, who loved me and gave Himself for me.' (Gal. ii. 20) Every day the Israelites required the water from the Rock in the dry and parched land, so the Christian daily drinks the truth of God. Christ is his daily refreshment. These are for our *weariness*. The Israelites likewise had Joshua to fight, and Moses to pray, against their foe Amalek; so we have the Spirit to war against the flesh, and we have our advocate with the Father. Christ presents the blood for us on high, and daily we require our feet to be washed from all earthly defilement. These are God's provisions for our *sin*.

Again, as to fact, we are in the *Canaan* conflict, following our Joshua through all his wars, which are our wars. Every Christian is really, as to fact, in Egypt, in the Wilderness, and in Canaan, at one and the same time. Different aspects may be more prominently ours at one time than at another, and this constitutes experience. The experience of Christians is not always Christian experience.

3. THE CHRISTIAN'S EXPERIENCE.

What do we find the every-day experience of Christians to be? According as a Christian understands what his standing is and what his state is, so will be his experience. But every Christian's experience must be 'a walking with God.' He may be, as to experience, sheltered by blood and hardly knowing it, like an Israelite in Egypt not realizing the safety that there was under the blood-sprinkled lintel. He may be consciously at peace with God by the blood, but still trembling under the fear of coming into condemnation, like an Israelite not seeing the path through the sea, and trembling lest Pharaoh's host should destroy him; but he will be walking with God up to the light he has. He may be rejoicing on the solid ground of Christ risen, having for ever done with all that was against him, and being conscious that God is now for him; and he thus walks with God, like an Israelite passed through the Red Sea, and entered upon the wilderness journey. And, finally, he may be walking as in heavenly places, like an Israelite who had passed through the Jordan and had settled in Canaan.

He is God's workmanship, and is now getting into the mystery of His will (Eph. i. 9), having lost sight of the thought of his own salvation, and being absorbed in God—as the aged pilgrims have told us that for years they had never had a thought about their own salvation—as the aged Bengel said, 'The same old terms.' And it is only when in conscious experience we have been taken thus far, that we can study God for His own sake—for what He is. This is the furthest we can reach here.

The *standing* of every believer before God in Christ Jesus, known only by faith here, is the same, and it is independent of his realising it or enjoying it.

The actual *state* of every Christian upon the earth is likewise the same. What an anomaly any Christian is in the world! A son of God walking through a God-hating world, with a God-hating devil its head, and having within him a God-hating nature; the fact being that every Christian, as to conflict down here, is in Egypt, in the Wilderness, and in Canaan.

The *experience* of every Christian is not the same, but varies in different people, and in the same person at different times, according as he knows his standing before God, knows his state, and walks in the Spirit. Thus we find the reason of so much seeming contradiction in Scripture, and in the writings of God-taught men. I am sometimes confronted with a passage in a man's writings, and asked, 'Do you believe that?'

'Yes,' I answer; 'and do you believe that?' —a directly opposite statement (seemingly), and again I say—

'Yes,' because I find the same expressions in God's Word.

They all reconcile themselves in our own consciousness, if we are submissive enough to wait and learn God's mind. I wish that you, my Christian reader, may distinctly see the difference between what the Christian is in God's sight, and what he is in this world, and also why there is so much difference in different Christians. There is one path, and but one path, in which our God and Father would have us walk; that is the path of His own Son here in conscious sonship, witnessing for Him as if we were in Egypt, in the Wilderness, and in Canaan, taking sides with Him against the world, against ourselves, and against the devil. This is Christian experience; but, alas! this is not always the experience of Christians. This may depend upon their not rightly dividing the word of truth, or their not seeing the truth in its many aspects. If we draw up a few seeming contradictions from God's word concerning the Christian in parallel columns, if we read down one of them we shall find the experience of some Christians; if again we read down the other we shall find the experience of another class of Christians; but Christian experience is the harmonious and scriptural blending of both. (I wonder what angels think as they see such sons of God here!) Did not Paul know this strange contradiction? I saw an infidel tract the other day, meant to prove the Bible to be false by drawing up in parallel columns about a dozen contradictions found in Scripture, such as, 'Whosoever is born of God sinneth not,' and, 'if we say we have no sin, we deceive ourselves,' &c; and I thought 'Are the infidels really so far back?' So I commend the following four dozen, instead of one, to their notice, and promise more when these are understood. The poor infidel never heard of a new creation and an old in the same man. He knows only the old, and tries to patch it.

Well-known.	Yet unknown.
Behold we live.	Dying.
Always rejoicing.	Yet sorrowful.
Making many rich.	Yet poor.
Possessing all things.	Having nothing.
Ye have put off the old man.	Put off all these.
Ye have put on the new man.	Put on therefore.
Who can be against us?	World, devil, and flesh.
Who shall lay anything to our charge?	The Accuser accuses the brethren day and night.
Who is he that condemneth?	We judge ourselves.
He that is born of God sinneth not.	If we say that we have no sin we deceive ourselves.
We are not in the flesh.	As long as we are in the flesh.
Not under law.	Keep my commandments.
He that believeth in the Son hath everlasting life.	We live if ye stand fast in the Lord.
The Lord's freemen.	Christ's Slaves.
Being made free from sin.	Blood cleanseth (not has cleansed) us from all sin.
Accepted in the Beloved.	We labour to be accepted (in service).
We are not in the flesh, but in the Spirit.	The flesh lusts against the spirit, and the spirit against the flesh.
God who always causeth us to triumph.	What great conflict I have for you.

We are already saved.	We are working out our salvation.
	We are waiting for salvation.
Let us therefore as many as be *perfect*.	Not as though I were already *perfect*.
Ye are *complete* in Him.	We pray that we may stand *complete* in all the will of God.
Seeing ye have *purified* your souls.	Let every one that hath this hope in Him *purify* himself.
Ye are *unleavened*.	Purge out the old *leaven*.
Father who hath made us *meet* to be partakers of the inheritance of the saints in light.	When He shall appear we shall be *like* Him.
Always confident.	With fear and trembling.
Through death he destroyed Him that had the power of death.	The last enemy that shall be destroyed is death.
Everywhere and in all things—	
To be full, and	To be hungry.
To abound, and	To suffer need. (Phil. iv. 12.)
Dead to sin	Let not sin therefore reign.
Risen with Christ.	Mortify therefore your members which are upon the earth.
I am strong.	When I am weak.
We have an anchor sure and steadfast.	Make your calling and election sure.
They shall never perish.	Lest I should be a castaway.
Why as though living in the world.	The life which we now live in the flesh.
I am dead.	Nevertheless I live.
We are sanctified, justified; Christ our sanctification.	We pray that we may be sanctified wholly.
Seated in heavenly places in Christ.	We are in the world.
Bear ye one another's burdens.	Every man shall bear his own burden.
Your bodies are the temples of the Holy Ghost.	I know that in me (that is, in my flesh) dwelleth no good thing.

Saved from sin.	Chief of sinners.
Justified by faith.	Justified by works.
Sanctified by blood and will of God.	Sanctified by the word and Spirit.
Saints by call.	Purified by progress.
We (Christians) shall not come into judgment.	We (Christians) must all appear before the judgment seat of Christ.

All these seeming contradictions are thoroughly explained when one sees the difference between our standing and our state. If I reckon my standing according to my state, I am in a low and God-dishonouring experience. If I bring the power and character of my standing to mould my state, then I shall have a happy and God-honouring experience.

The Lamb on the cross has purchased all.	The Lamb from the throne, when He returns in power shall claim all, and actually take all.
In Egypt it is the blood of the Lamb.	Romans and Galatians shew us the power that brought us out and keeps us in Egypt.
In Amalek's fight it is the blood of the Lamb who is the Advocate on high, that is presented.	Hebrews looks at the Christian as always in the Wilderness.
It is by the blood of the Lamb that the accuser of the brethren is overcome. Clad in God's armour we fight.	Ephesians is the book of our Canaan.

Soon faith will be fact. May our blessed Lord grant it. Not at death will this be true of the whole Church of God, but when He returns. Our experience will then be according both to faith and to fact; our state shall then be as our standing;

our standing shall be as our state. We shall then be 'like Him,' soul and body. Do we not 'ong for the time when the last member of the Church shall be under the shelter of the blood-sprinkled lintel, and we shall be caught up together from a doomed *world*,—when the last conflict with Amalek shall have been fought, and his remembrance blotted out for ever; the *flesh* for ever left; 'sins and iniquities remembered no more for ever;' when the accuser of the brethren shall have been cast out of the heavenly place, and every opposing *spiritual wickedness* shall have been routed; when our Joshua, by His judgment-warfare (Rev. iv. to xxii.), shall have cleared the inheritance? Then, in the splendour of the Lamb on the throne, we shall be manifested as the sons of God.

Fellow Christian, are you making your experience the standard for your walk? This is wrong.

Are you making your state your standard? This also is wrong.

God would have us make our standing our standard. This honours Him. This gives conquering power.

Our attitude now is to wait calmly for the hour when all shall be our own in fact and also in experience, which is now ours in faith only; when our standing will be our state. Even the Apostle Paul has not yet all; he is waiting with the Lord for what he was waiting for while here,—'not to be unclothed, but clothed upon, that mortality might be swallowed up of life.' (2 Cor. v.) This is why resurrection, not death, is our hope—why we wait for the Lord's coming to us, and not for our going to Him. We do not wait for happiness merely, we wait for what will bring to a close this great paradox between *standing* and *state*, and also terminate that unseen state of disembodied souls with the Lord in Paradise. 'Even so, come, Lord Jesus.' 'Beloved, now are we the sons of God; and it doth not yet appear what we shall be; but we know that when He shall appear, we shall be LIKE HIM; for we shall see Him as He is. And every one that hath this hope in Him purifieth himself, even as He is pure.' (1 John iii. 2.)

The world, the devil, and the flesh give you conflict. The Father, the Son, and the Holy Ghost give you triumph.

PRAISE the Lord with hearts and voices,
    Gathered in His holy name;
Every quicken'd soul rejoices,
    Hearing of the Saviour's fame.

Praise the living God who gave us,
    Lost and ruin'd as we lay,
His beloved Son to save us,
    Bearing all our sin away.

Praise the Lord for all His guiding,
    Snares so thickly round us lie;
We in His own light abiding,
    Are directed by His eye.

Praise Him for His long forbearance,
    How our sin His heart must pain;
Righteous is His loving-kindness,
    Cleansing us from every stain.

Praise Him, enemies assail us,
   As we through the desert go;
But His sword can never fail us,
   It shall silence every foe.

Praise Him for the manna given,
   Falling freshly every day;
Jesus Christ our Lord from Heaven,
   Is our food through all the way.

Praise Him for the water flowing,
   Freely in its boundless tide;
Christ the smitten Rock we're knowing,
   Pierced for us His wounded side.

Praise Him through the desert marchin
   Onward to the golden shore;
For our Saviour we are watching,
   And we'll praise Him evermore.

'Under the Sun.'

OUR WALK.

ECCLESIASTES.

ON reading the book of Ecclesiastes I have been struck with the frequent occurrence of this expression, '*Under the sun.*' It occurs twenty-nine times in this book of ten chapters, and is nowhere else in the Bible. 'Under the heavens' is thrice mentioned, and 'upon the earth' four times.

I have met Christians who have been sadly perplexed by several expressions in this book, which seem so contradictory to other parts of the Scripture. Infidels have also exultingly brought some of its detached sentences as sanctioning their blasphemies. Legalists and Unitarians have quoted some of its precepts as proving their man-exalting and God-dishonouring doctrines. Worldly professors use its verses as a warrant for their worldliness, and an excuse for their practices.

That expression, '*under the sun,*' is the thread on which the whole book is crystallized. If we remember this, we shall have not the slightest difficulty in meeting infidel opposition or world-hearted profession. Solomon was the wisest as he was the richest king, trying all that was 'under the sun.' The Holy Spirit has, in these few chapters, with divine accuracy given us his experience, and 'what can the man do that cometh after the king?' He had plenty of money and all the resources where men think pleasure is to be found 'under the sun'—wine, music, works, vineyards, gardens, orchards, fruit trees, waterpools, servants, possessions of cattle, silver, gold, peculiar treasures, men-singers, women-singers, musical instruments of all sorts—in short, whatever his eyes desired he kept not from them (chap. ii.) A better collection could not be brought together for any man 'under the sun.'

And with all his enjoyment he still kept his wisdom, as he says, 'yet acquainting mine heart with wisdom.' But in such multiplied sources of pleasure did he not tarry too long at the enjoyment of one side of his nature, and leave some other corner untried? Nay; he found a season for everything. For loving, for hating, for laughing, for weeping, for dancing, for mourning, for all he had a time. He saw that after all he had tried *under the sun* he was no better than a beast; for as we look at a man and a beast *under the sun,* a common grave shuts out the light of the sun equally from the horse and from his rider.

It is *under the sun* that the outward eye sees, and if the things seen are all that we are to have, there is nothing better than what Solomon says—'Behold that which I have *seen:* it is good and comely to eat and to drink, and to enjoy the good of all his labour that he taketh under the sun all the days of his life, which God giveth him; for it is his *portion*.' The *things seen* give eating, drinking, and enjoyment of labour as the only portion. This is the highest good, according to what was seen by the greatest philosopher as looking at things '*under the sun.*' He was also a great student. Read 1 Kings iv. 33.

As to the higher part of man, we find a wonderful text in Eccl. ix. 1 : 'No man knoweth either love or hatred by all that is before him.' No; we have to look *above* us for love and hatred, not *before* us, that is to say in this world. By what is before us we are asked to remember our Creator, but are never turned to our Redeemer. Hence, '*under the sun*,' we find men scarcely dare rise above the names Creator, Providence. And when we do remember this great Creator, as creatures under His sun, we find that the conclusion of all, the ultimate limit we can reach, is to know His demands upon us; as His demands are known in their own place and nature on a tree or an animal. His demand on us as creatures, —the whole duty of man, which no man ever did or can do, is to 'fear God and keep His commandments.'

This wisest and richest man found '*under the sun*' no profit in all his labour; nothing new; wicked men in judgment; oppression of the right; folly and wisdom going to the same end; chance seeming to regulate all; many sore evils consequent, notwithstanding what he says in 1 Kings v. 4: 'The Lord my God hath given me rest on every side, so that there is neither adversary nor evil occurrent.' In short, he found the beginning vanity, the middle vanity, the end vanity. The sum of all '*under the sun*,'—vanity of vanities.

How complete is the change when we turn to contemplate Him who comes from far above the sun, who created the sun and the earth, and descended to the earth from His rainbow-circled throne. When Christ came, He did not reveal the name 'Creator,' it was the name 'Father.' Christ was the last test of all '*under the sun.*' The whole world has now been brought in guilty before God. Man's duty was to receive Christ, instead of which he gave Him a cross.

God is love, and God was manifest in the flesh; perfect love, perfect light. Eternal life has been here from above the sun. Hatred against sin has been seen, as nowhere else it can be seen, when, made sin for us, the sinless One drained the cup of the wrath of God. Love for the sinner has been seen, as nowhere else it can be seen, in that 'God so loved the world that He gave His only-begotten Son, that whosoever believeth in Him should not perish, but have everlasting life.'

A sister who had realized her position as witnessing for Christ, and had come to understand what is meant by Solomon's time for everything 'under the sun,' wrote about a marriage party at which she had to be present. After describing

what happened, she said, 'We then left
early, leaving the gay party to practise Sol...

We that have believed in the Son have
most strange and anomalous position 'under
sun.' 'As He is, so are we in this world.' A
Son of man dead, risen, and now in heave
the fulness of His Father's love, so are we in
world. We have nothing whatever to do
what is 'under the sun,' beyond getting thr
this world as simply as possible. 'If ye the
risen with Christ, seek those things which
above, where Christ sitteth on the right han
God. Set your affection (it is literally *mind*
in the passage 'who *mind* earthly things'
things *above*—*not* on things on the earth, for
are dead, and your life is hid with Christ in G
All this is intended to draw us away from v
is under the sun to what is *above*, even to
Lord Himself. What is the occasion of all
worldly walk of so many professing Christi
We are not asking what the originating cause
There is a difference between the originating ca
and the occasion, sometimes called the predisp
ing and the exciting causes. The originating
predisposing cause is found in this, that all Ch
tians have in them the old Adam nature,
changed and unchangeable, which lusts against
new, which abhors the things unseen and
walk by faith, which feeds upon the things s
feasts on and revels in this present world.
there are several occasions or exciting ca
which stir up this old nature into conformity

the world. Let us look at three of the chief occasions of worldliness:

1st, Ignorance of self.
2d, Ignorance of what the world is.
3d, Ignorance of what God says about the world.

1. IGNORANCE OF SELF.

When Christians do not realise that their own Adam natures still in them are inclined to worldliness, they are very apt to become worldly. They come nearer and nearer to the world, thinking themselves safe, and still doing nothing wrong, not knowing that it is like bringing gunpowder near the fire. If Christians would realise that they have a nature within them that feeds upon God's dishonour, they would be more watchful and prayerful. Every Christian has within him a traitor which loves the world, its ways and its principles, in some shape or other; a traitor which, but for the power of an ever-present Spirit, would surrender the keys of the citadel at once to the world outside; a traitor which is not subject to the law of God, nor indeed can be; a traitor which is not to be trifled with, far less trusted; a traitor which is ever planning and scheming for its own gratification, and which is capable of anything evil. Christian! watch and pray against this foe within, as well as against foes without. Every Christian has the flesh still within him, which is a traitor against God.

II. IGNORANCE OF WHAT THE WORLD IS.

When we do not know what 'the world' is, we are very prone to slip into worldliness before we are aware. Some profess not to be clear upon what is worldly. They know well enough, however, the meaning of getting on in 'the world.' Some look at '*the world*' as that which is glaringly wicked, or God-dishonouring in other people. The poor man speaks of the rich man in his grand house, or the great man who never thinks of God, as being in the world. Such may be the case, but every man has his '*world*' into which he is tempted to go: the meanest as well as the greatest, the most secluded as well as those in the centre of a great city. A pretty ribbon or a new dress, a good dinner or a nice party, may be as much '*the world*' as the gayest and most fashionable assembly.

Often the question is asked, Is it right to go here or there? to do this or that? Is this of '*the world*' or not? God has given us a perfect criterion: 'All that is in the world . . . . is not of the Father, but is of the world.' This makes all plain to a child with the Father. Is this of the Father? If not, it is of the world. How well every Christian understands this in some measure! Does the size of your world not increase just in proportion as you know the Father? Things are now classed under the title '*world*,' that were not thought to be worldly when we started in the race. The road gets narrower as this thing and the other thing are seen to be of '*the world*,' till we find ourselves walking in the lonely path with the lonely One.

Fellow-Christian, do you not see something this year to be of '*the world*' that you did not see last year? Have you been thus learning the Father? Is it a sign that the Father is being known more when we hear of professing Christians, yes, even deacons, elders, pastors, countenancing the worldly meeting, the gay assembly, or the dancing party? And where is the harm? is asked by many a voice. Ask at the entrance of many a fashionable gathering, '*Is this of the Father?*' and you will get the contempt that your presence there deserves. For the world loves and knows its own; your presence asking such a question, would be an intrusion.

This spirit of the world is paralysing the whole of Christian energy, as it is leavening the whole of Christendom. No wonder that there is a slumber as of death over our land, an unaccountable nightmare resting on the spirits of many Christian men, a feeling that we are just at the awful pause before some fearful explosion. Christians take the world's ways and party strifes in its politics and rule, blunting the edge of their spiritual nature, hardening their consciences, condescending to mingle in the world's battles. Let the potsherds of earth strive with the potsherds thereof. Where are the garments unspotted by the world? Christians also are mixed up with the world's company, sitting at the world's table, happy with the world's joys and jokes, singing the world's songs, and their bleeding Lord hanging at their side, each worldly thought or action doing dishonour to Him.

Young disciples, (the 'little children' or babes of 1 John ii. 13) are especially liable to be carried away with the cultivated, respectable, educated, quiet, polite, agreeable, pleasant, worldly companion. Young disciples, in the name of Him who hung on Calvary for you, keep no company with any unconverted person. You may have to meet them at school or in business, but never keep company with them. 'Come out from among them and be ye separate.' A young disciple was once asked concerning a companion.

'Well, was she a friend or an enemy?'

'In what way?'

'A friend or an enemy to Christ?'

'I really could not say.'

'But you know that all are either friends or foes? there is not a third company. Is she converted?'

'I don't think so.'

'Then, of course, we know to whom she belongs. Let us be friends to all the Lord's friends, and enemies to all His enemies—loving them, praying for them, and trying to get them converted, but coming out from among them, and being separate.' My brother, will that cross, will that bleeding One, not draw thy thoughts, thy words, thyself, away from this cruel world? Let them quaff their wine, let them chorus the revel song, let them have their time to dance. They are '*under the sun.*' '*Under the sun*' He died for thee.

That sun was darkened when He was thinking of thee. He loved thee. Thy name, as an individual, was in His omniscient mind, when in darkness and agony He was forsaken of His God. Nails and a cross never kept Him there. He Himself made that iron and that wood, but love kept Him on the cross. Thou hast said, 'He loved me, and gave Himself for me.' His cross, His grave, separate thee from '*the world*,' as they separate thee from thy sins. Dost thou realise that every unconverted man is reckoned by thy Lord as a murderer? that this world is under the charge of murdering the Son of God?

In this land, at this moment, it is difficult to know the *church* from the *world*. The world, 'of the earth, earthy,' has said to the Church, the bride of the Lamb, of the heavens, 'heavenly,' 'Come a little down to us, and we will rise a little up to you, and we can shake hands and agree.' This in the present day is called *liberality, charity, large-heartedness,* and he who dares to dissent is called a bigot, one of peculiar views, a man of extremes.

'The world' makes its social gathering and invites the Christian. A compromise is effected. The Christian leaves at home his peculiar testimony for his rejected Lord. 'The world' lays aside a little of its open worldliness, and they thus agree. 'The world' has been raised somewhat. Its tone has been elevated. The Christian has come down from his high standing ground, and has lost his place as the separated one—His

Lord is dishonoured, and this is modern[...] ity! The world and the Christian a[gree;] God's name, God's glory, the offence of t[he...] are given up as the price of the agreement!

Yea, some have shown their ignoran[ce and] heartlessness so much as to bring in C[hrist's] example, and make His conduct a cloak for [their] worldliness, and the Holy Jesus a minister [of sin.] True, no one was ever such a friend to the [sinner] as *He*, and no one was so separate from sin[ners.] Did He contract any defilement by sitting [and] eating with sinners? It would be blasphe[my to] think it. Can you perfectly manifest Christ w[her]ever you go? But the rule here, as everyw[here,] is perfect and simple, 'Whether therefore ye [eat] or drink, or whatsoever ye do, do all to the [glory] of God.' (1 Cor. x. 31.) Do you keep comp[any] with that friend because it is for the glory of G[od?] Do you accept that invitation to dinner bec[ause] it is for the glory of God? or not rather bec[ause] you will enjoy it, and perhaps meet some one [you] like, or something else for you. And is [this] following the Lord Jesus? Not a word did [He] speak, not a thought did He think, not a step [did] He take, but was for God's glory. Not a comp[any] He entered, but this was His *only* reason for go[ing.] Is it yours? Let conscience answer. An[d if] you can go on with worldly people and in wor[ldly] ways, either you will reap daily and bitter sor[row,] and have to come in broken and contrite spir[it to] the footstool of grace, or you have no hear[t for] the crucified One. You know not the Christ w[ho]

You are not Christ's one.
Christian!

...day there is nothing that is
...Christendom more evidently than this
...worldly policy, worldly ways of ad-
...cause of Christ, worldly principles,
...xims, worldly motives, worldly vindi-
...conduct, worldly schemes and artifices
...employed; and worldly arguments are
...duced to shew that all such are quite in
...

...of competition, which is 'the life of
...been adopted in those un-Christlike
...in the Church of the living God. Arti-
...trickery with world-shows, bazaars, and
...are used to extract money from the
...willing and unwilling victims to
...God's kingdom! the Lord all the time
...cheerful giver. But cheerful, or not
...the worldly church principle is, the
...be obtained! Read *Babylon's great*
...Revelations xviii. 12 and 13—*gold* at
...of the list, *souls of men* at the foot—not
...like what may be seen in Christianised

...mixture of world and church of this
...century in Britain, who could discern
...of the Crucified One? Everything
...comfortably. There is little of the taking
...cross;' many excuses for conformity
...world.

...not very long ago of one who, standing

very high in 'the Church' as a leading and devoted Christian, at a marriage party publicly announced that such a season was for enjoyment, and that such enjoyment should take the form of singing songs, &c.; holy hymns and such-like were not appropriate. Certainly it was the time for enjoyment. And if 'any man is merry, *let him sing psalms.*' But this does not suit modern mixtures of 'Church' and 'world,' fashionable Christianity!

Religion, with its psalms and hymns and spiritual songs, may do all very well for Sunday; for solemn times; for deaths or for funerals, for prayers, morning and night, at family worship; but for enjoyment, for merry-making, let us have a worldly song, or some foolish love-sonnet, before all the means that God has ordained as channels for our joy!

This is what is called *intelligent* Christianity. 'Rejoice' is the motto of such men, but they forget '*in the Lord.*' Man's songs, man's dancing, are their channels of joy—'psalms, hymns, and spiritual songs,' God's channel. The judgment-day will try all. Beloved fellow-Christian, rejoice *now* in such wise that you would look back from your death-bed with satisfaction and say, 'It was not of the world.'

In travelling by rail, take out your Bible and quietly begin to read for your own instruction, in the presence of your fellow-passengers, and you will quickly observe that eyes are upon you in strange wonder—the eyes of those, too, who wish

..., but who cannot under-
... who reads the Bible for *enjoyment*.
... they think, should be read as a duty;
... trash, in the shape of some yellow-
... or some new article of man's folly,
... more palatable and enjoyable. Dear
... you getting much enjoyment from the
... of the Word of your Father? This
... with His ideas, and displace your
... will show you that there is much
... *the world*' than perhaps you dreamt of;
... '*under the sun*' is equally vain for in-
... or for enjoyment. This leads us to the
... of the third occasion of this most
... and painful, though too common spec-
... worldliness in a Christian.

...ORANCE OF WHAT GOD SAYS ABOUT THE WORLD.

... knows the world thoroughly. There
... words in Scripture translated world;
... (κοσμος), which literally means the
... its perfect order and arrangement, as
... chaos; 2nd, Aion (αιων), which literally
... period of time, an age; and 3rd, Oikou-
... (οικουμενη), literally meaning the inhabited
... world.

... with the two first have we at present
... What could be more beautiful than the
... of this perfectly ordered world—the
... that God brought out of chaos? The
... this sense, in itself is not evil; but its

rightful Lord has been crucified; and
this age, or dispensation, or period of
all must be away from God. By
things in heaven and in earth shall be
under the one head, Christ, when the
beautiful world, will appear in purer
in its pristine beauty, when it will be
present age, but the day of the Son of
age to come.' (Heb. ii. 5.) Meanwhile
of the serpent defiles all. Its beautiful
mountains, and plains, are polluted by
sence of men in rebellion against a holy
the unavenged blood of its martyred Lord
on it calling aloud for vengeance.

When the Spirit of God begins the
exhortation to the Romans, in the 12th
the first command of detail, after present
bodies living sacrifices, is, 'Be not conf
this world;' that is, 'be not conformed
age.' Until a man knows this foundation
he cannot go on to the other related du
done with the spirit of the age. Why?
the age is under Satan, who is the god of
(2 Cor. iv. 4.) Its rulers are the rulers of
ness of this age. (Eph. vi. 12.) And Chri
Himself for our sins, that He might deli
from this present evil age, according to
of God and our Father.' (Gal. i. 4.) De
sook Paul because he 'loved this presen
(2 Tim. iv. 10); and earth's wisdom is
study of the Christian, for we do not speak

wisdom of this age, nor of the princes of this age. (1 Cor. ii. 6.)

Christ our Lord and Saviour alone we own to be King of kings, but in this age the devil is prince of this world (John xvi. 11); and he declared this to Christ, the only true KING, in Matt. iv. 8, when he said he would give Him all the kingdoms of the world. The Creator was in the world made by Him, and the world did not know Him, but hated and crucified Him. The wisdom of this world is foolishness with God, and its power, weakness. 'We have received not the spirit of the world, but the Spirit which is of God.' (1 Cor. ii.) And God has chosen the foolish things, the weak things, the base things of this world as His own vessels.

My reader listen to God's own word—' Know ye not that the friendship of the world is enmity with God? whosoever, therefore, will be a friend of the world is the enemy of God.' (James iv. 4.) 'Love not the world, neither the things that are in the world. If any man love the world, the love of the Father is not in him.' (1 John ii. 15.) A man is known by the company he keeps, by the books he enjoys. Do you not enjoy a nice worldly dinner-party where there is nothing very evil done, but all the events of the world are discussed, much better than attending two or three prayer or worship meetings in a week? Have you made choice of the alternative? The love of the Father is not in you. ' They are of the world, therefore speak they of the world, and the world heareth

them.' (1 John iv. 5.) 'We know [that we are of]
God, and the whole world lieth in the [wicked one.]'
(1 John v. 19.)

My reader, pause and think. Are [you deceiv]-
ing yourself? Do you love *the world*[? If so,]
before God, you cannot deny it, then [the love of]
the Father is not in you. You go to ch[urch, you]
are very respectable on Sundays and w[eek-days,]
you are honest, and charitable, and kind, [but you]
love the world. Your feasts and solemn [days are]
an abomination unto God. You cann[ot force]
yourself to hate the world. It is natural [to love]
it. By your love you prove that you h[ave not]
the nature in you that abhors the worl[d, and,]
therefore, you have not been born again, [but have]
been deceiving yourself. I would solem[nly ad]-
vise you, before God, to start from the b[eginning]
by getting converted. Cain was the fi[rst man]
to make the world comfortable apart fr[om God.]
God made him a vagabond. He built a ci[ty. He]
was the father of all the great world-im[provers,]
with their harps and organs. No doubt [they]
made themselves very happy; no doubt [despised]
their music and dancing; perhaps cari[catured]
the dying words of Abel, or the takin[g up of]
Enoch, like the 'Messiah' and 'Elijah' [of our]
days. Having considered these occa[sions of]
worldliness, let us consider—

IV. THE PLACE OF A CHRISTIAN UNDER T[HE]

Read John xvii., and there you find—
First. At verse 9, Christ says, 'I pray

… for them which Thou hast *given*
… by the Father to Christ, we Chris-
… separated from this world by the eternal
… Father, and by the intercessory prayer
… Mingling with the world, we break
… that wondrous chain that Christ became a
… ; we do despite to the Father's pur-
… trample on the prayers of the Son.

… In verses 11 and 15 we are spoken of
… the world: 'I am no more in the world,
… are in the world.' And as He is, so are
… we living His life, reproducing Christ
… those that are left to do so? He was the
… here; we are the light of the world
… His absence. Brother, did you ever feel
… because the Lord Jesus is not here, because
… been left? Are you mingling with the
… You do dishonour to that heart which
… on your love while left here.

… *Hated* by the world: 'The world
… them,' because the world hated Him.
… Christians are persecuted for their own sake,
… for righteousness' sake. Christians may
… for their own disagreeable ways; but are
… for your likeness to Christ? He said,
… hated Me without a cause.' Do they hate
… because you manifest His holy name?
… you mingling with the world? If so, you
… to escape the hatred, yea, you are
… consenting that the world did right in
… your gracious Redeemer.

… '*Not of* the world,' verses 14 and 16.

This is the cause of the former.' T[...]
its own. We are citizens of heaven. [...]
our Fatherland. Heaven is our home[...]
is our metropolis. We are foreigners h[...]
are like the Abyssinian captives while the[...]
the chains of the African king. A few [...]
more, and, beloved fellow-captive, the ch[...]
fall, and we shall neither be in nor of [...]
We are not of it, just as the Lord Jesus [...]
of it. A homeless, lonely stranger, the [...]
journer had 'not where to lay his head.' As [...]
in Phil. iii. 20—the epistle which gives us Ch[...]
experience—' Our conversation,' or more [...]
our citizenship, or commonwealth, is in [...]
from whence we look for the Saviour the [...]
Jesus Christ.

We are here under protest. We protest [...]
the awful power that the world-rulers have [...]
in former days, and not one of whom has [...]
protested against, namely, Pilate's boast, '[...]
power to crucify Thee.' We glory in this [...]
we are identified with the murdered Man. [...]
you mingling with the world? By so doing [...]
are denying your Fatherland, you are asha[...]
your citizenship.

Fifth. Ver. 15. While left in this wor[...]
are *kept* from the evil in it. Are we to rush [...]
the evil from which our blessed Lord prayed [...]
Father we might be *kept?* Are we to [...]
through a Father's love, a Father's watchful [...]
and join the ranks of the aliens? Do we search [...]
broken cistern, and thirst again for more [...]

…… dancing '*under the sun*,' while
…… that are '*kept?*' Tremendous evil!
…… tremendous because, unseen and un-
…… is around us, and from it we have to
…… Nothing but our Lord's constant prayer,
…… Father's constant, untiring love, could
……

Ver. 18. We are *sent* into the world.
…… was sent, so are we. We must be out
…… before we can be sent into it. The
…… us out of the world. We were crucified
…… In resurrection-life we are sent back to it,
…… as specimens of saved sinners, resurrec-
……, stranger-witnesses, men that cannot be
……, men whose life is hid with Christ in
…… Are you mingling with what is '*under the*
……' If so, you deny the resurrection of Christ
…… resurrection with Him, and that you are
…… into the world, and have to maintain your
…… as one who has been thus sent.

Ver. 20. We are to *preach* to the
…… All that are to be saved will be so by the
…… mentality of saved men, sinners like them-
…… carrying the word of life to the dead.
…… a strange infatuation in the minds of
…… that because we are in the world to do
…… work, therefore we must become some-
…… assimilated to the world in order to get
…… level! But the Christian is a 'light,'
…… does not do its work by assimilation with
……, but by opposition to it. The Christian's
…… carrying the Word to a dead world is

not in becoming like the dead, but in
his new life, going to dead sinners with
potence of God, and preaching His gospel
and resurrection, not schemes of reform
anything else except this gospel, knowing
the 'gospel is the power of God.' The Ch
wisdom is not that which schemes and
success according to worldly tactics; but
direct opposition to all, seeming to be d
foolishness. Saul's armour looks very
David's sling and stone seem quite contem

We do our duty to the world only as we
our Nazarite or separated character. We
brightly only as we oppose the darkness
benefit mankind only as we glorify God
testify for the Crucified One. We are
by man and chastened of God if we mingle
the world and 'blow hot and cold.' Christ
out of His mouth the lukewarm.

'I am not a man of extremes,' says the
ideal of modern fashionable Christianity.
you were either cold or hot,' says God,
God be true, and every man a liar.'

Let us 'make the best of both worlds
man. 'If any man love the world, the l
the Father is not in him,' says God.

'Secure friends here, and still keep a h
heaven hereafter,' says man. 'The friends
the world is enmity with God,' says God.

'Let us take our time for everything
"*under the sun*,"—dancing, laughter, amuse
comfort, position,' is man's creed. 'If an

... Me, let him deny himself, and take
... and follow Me, is what God says,
... you shall reap.
... the light is sweet, and a pleasant thing
... the eyes to behold the sun; but if a man
... years, and rejoice in them all, yet let
... remember the days of darkness, for they shall
... All that cometh is vanity. Rejoice,
... man, in thy youth; and let thy heart
... thee in the days of thy youth, and walk in
... of thine heart, and in the sight of thine
... but know thou, that for all these things
... will bring thee into judgment.' (Eccles. xi.
... Man, who shall live for ever, giving up
... eternity for present pleasure, giving up Christ
... world, is like one who is colour-blind, that
... a person who though he can see well
... his way through the world, cannot dis-
... between red and green, or any other of
... beautiful hues that are seen in the rainbow.
... that see colour in all its beauty and diver-
... God has made it, cannot but think it a
... misfortune for those who cannot distinguish
... colour from another. To them the crocus
... snowdrop appear the same as the green
... and it again as the stone wall. Everything
... is either black or white, and the glorious
... is not distinguished from the black cloud
... spans. Everything is to them like an
... and the lilies of the field, which we
... to consider, have no more beauty than
... from their shape and position. It is a

misfortune, but the unfortunate one does not [feel?] his loss. How true is that saying of Sir J. Herschel, referring to this colour-blindness, '*What we never knew we never missed*.' How true in the great realities of our existence! How many people go about this world absorbed in its business, its pleasure, or its science, and have never seen the most glorious sight that ever shone upon it—the perfect love of God to sinners, and the perfect hatred of God against sin; or rather, have never seen the most glorious Person that ever trod this earth, as the sacrifice for their sins, as their propitiation, as the object to fill their hearts now and for ever!

They never knew Him, and they never missed Him. If you were saying, 'Christ is not in the world, do you miss Him?' The idea would startle many. Others would feel that they would not at all like Him to be always with them; they would not feel free if He were always sitting at their table, or went with them wherever they went. Have you never heard people say, when a godly man had left their company, 'Well, I am glad he's gone; we couldn't do anything before him?' How would you like Christ to be always beside you? Far from missing Him, you are really very glad He is not here. Thank God there are those who have known Him, that do miss Him, and are waiting for Him. Why does the lady of the world so enjoy company, while the pierced Christ is never missed? Because she never knew Him. Why do the men of the world enjoy their life

…… or their pleasure, and do not miss …… greatest gift? Because they never …… They wonder that people can enjoy …… meetings, gospel preachings, or Bible-read- …… always enjoy them—ready for them in …… at noon, or evening. They pity such. …… like the man who is colour-blind, pitying …… we stand in rapt enjoyment admiring the …… rainbow? He feels the rain falling, but …… and admire no rainbow. We see the …… colouring of the rainbow, and forget …… They never knew the joy of being the …… therefore they never miss it. And what …… in the world after Christ is taken away? …… was here, and God looked on Him, well- …… ; but man in his blindness crucified this …… worthy object on earth, and what is left? …… told us 'All that is in the world'—

…… 'The Lust of the Flesh.'

…… 'The Lust of the Eye,' and—

…… 'The Pride of Life.' There are no other …… powers in the world but these. This …… is reigning in power to-day as in the days …… the Apostle.

…… '*The Lust of the Flesh.*' This has to do …… things by which the senses, taste and …… and all merely animal gratifications, are …… This is the lowest and most universal. …… poor equally are under its power. …… we eat, what shall we drink? Such …… eat to live, they live to eat, to enjoy them- …… satisfy all the fleshly lusts that war

against the soul. Thus we read of
'walk after the flesh, in the lust of
who serve 'divers lusts,' lewdness,
This is why tipplers and drunkards
world till they forget name, business,
family, body and soul, for drink, whi
front door admitting to every other
flesh. A man may be under the lust of
who is not a drunkard, but who wishes
himself on this side of his nature.

2d. '*The Lust of the Eye.*'—This
with the senses of seeing, hearing, and
Here the man has not only desires, but
gratify them. What shall we see?
thing, some new Vanity Fair. The A
would listen to anything new—quite
this lust of the eye. This is the second
power in the world. What will please
and tickle the ear? This is what finds its
satisfied in theatres, pantomimes, operas,
sentimental and comic songs. They are
one class: some thing that will satisfy
powers of *investigation* as the lust of the
has to do with the senses of *enjoyment*.
even carried into the worship of the church
what is ritualism but the lust of the eye?
lust of the eye is here gratified with gor
dresses, childish paraphernalia, sacred imit
of a pantomime, all accompanied by the
notes of worship performed on a splendid
solemn machine for making sound, worship
by proxy, to which the worshipper listen

… another, and for which he pays. … people, conclusively to prove it, say, … enjoy it.' Of course. The lust of the … the eye gratified. 'But wasn't the … entertaining and grand?' Of course, … ver Satan fails to make such things … he must try something else for the lust … 'Turn away mine eyes from behold… .' (Ps. cxix. 37.)

'*The Pride of Life*.'—This is not what shall … nor what shall we drink? nor what shall … But how shall we be seen? Where… shall we be clothed? What is the modern … party, and even a good deal of modern … going? Either the lust of the eye or the … life—either the lust to *see* or *to be seen*. … I be thought great? How can I make … in the world? How grand can my parties … ing all others? This requires, seeks, and … the opportunities for display. How can … the pinnacle of earth's fame? How can … great scholar? How can I be a great … ? How can I be anything great? I … such and such great men. I know Lord … , and am intimate with Lady so-and-so. … are some of the sentences of 'the pride of … Bengel says this pride of life 'is that which … lust abroad, and diffuses it more largely … world, so that a man *wishes to be as* … *possible*, in goods, in dress, in plate, in … in buildings, in estates, in servants, in … , *in* his equipage, in his offices.'

Is not one or other of these the key to the heart of every man in the world? And is not what all your friends, relatives, and all, by nature, have pleasure in? Perhaps not like one, but they will have another. How am I to get out of it? As long as I am 'of the world,' I cannot but get what is in the world. God says there is nothing in the world but this. You say you have Christ. Is He enough? If you ask such a question, you never knew Him; you do not miss Him. Suppose the lust of the flesh, the lust of the eye, the pride of life, out of the world. I guarantee that its votaries would miss them. Suppose good dinners, good parties, good theatres, thrilling novels, and worldly amusements, and greatness in some part of the world, were gone, many would miss them, and be miserable without them. But they are all doomed, and all that enjoy them. 'The world passeth away, and the lust thereof, but he that doeth the will of God abideth for ever.'

Let us see how man got this threefold cord bound round him, and how he is to get it broken. He got it in the first Adam. It is broken when he gets into the last Adam; then, he is not of the world nor of what is in it.

THE FIRST MAN'S FAILURE.

(Introducing the principles of the world.)

1st, 'The tree was good for food.' This is the *lust of the flesh.*

... the eyes.' This was the *lust*
...
... to be desired to make one wise.'
... *pride of life.*

THE SECOND MAN'S VICTORY.

(*overcoming the god of this world.*)

... Command that these stones be made
... This was the *lust of the flesh*, overcome
... 'Man shall not live by bread alone,
... every word that proceedeth out of the
... God.'

... The Devil sheweth him all the kingdoms
... world, and the glory of them, and saith
... all these things will I give Thee if Thou
... down and worship me.' This was the
... the eye, overcome by the Word, 'Thou
... worship the Lord thy God, and him only
... serve.'

... being set on a pinnacle of the temple.
... thyself down: for it is written He shall
... his angels charge concerning Thee.' This
... pride of life, overcome by that Word,
... shalt not tempt the Lord thy God.'

... is the victory that overcometh the world,
... our faith.' We live upon what is unseen.
... our time now, we say to the worldling. Go
... the world with all it has, the lust of the
... the lust of the eye, and the pride of life. It
... heaven you will ever see. We can well
... time, for this is all the hell we shall ever
... especially to young disciples is the ex-

'No Confidence in the Flesh.'

OUR SANCTIFICATION.

'DO you know what in a Government would deserve a vote of *want of confidence?*'

'Indeed, I have little to say in politics on one side or the other, but there is a government against which I would with all my heart give a vote of *no confidence.*'

'What is that?'

'The government of an evil heart within, which is ever striving for the reins of power.'

'I agree with you; this is first: self-government is man's first duty.'

'I find that the evil heart, or " the flesh," as it is called in Scripture, is branded by the Holy Ghost with this mark, "No confidence." Look at Phil. iii. 3. Three steps may be seen in that wonderful passage—

1st, Worship God in the Spirit;
2d, Rejoice in Christ Jesus;
3d, Have no confidence in the flesh.

God is seeking worshippers—those who can worship Him in spirit and in truth. This is no legal drudgery, nor one of the vain attempts of men to get into favour with God. You hear people, converted and unconverted, speaking of going to worship God. How could an unconverted man worship in spirit and in truth, when he neither has the Spirit in him nor has come to the Truth? and this alone is true worship. It is no mere routine of Christian duties—singing, praying, preaching, or hearing; but it is the outflow of heartfelt adoration to God—it may be in silence or in song or thanksgiving, but it is giving God back something, giving back His own gift, thinking God's thoughts about Christ.'

'And how can this high step be reached?'

'The Spirit's method is by making us "rejoice in Christ Jesus." No man can worship acceptably unless his joy is in Christ Jesus. In fact, worship is the overflow back to God of the full cup of joy. Why is there so little true worship? Because there is so little rejoicing in Christ Jesus. I know some are considered great authorities who would hardly dare to say they are saved, and call it presumption in those who do so; and I have often wondered what such think of this text, "Rejoice in Christ Jesus." A brother truly remarked that many Christians' Bibles should be printed, "Mourn in the Lord always; and again I say, mourn." "Rejoice in the Lord alway" is a most blessed exhortation given to us by Him who as the judge of all the earth might have justly condemned us, but who has laid the foundation of eternal joy in the blood of His cross.'

'But (you ask) do *you* always rejoice?'

'Now this is a very common mode of getting away from the authority of God, by comparing ourselves with one another instead of bowing to

God's word. Alas! no, I do not rejoice always; but when I do not, I have to confess it as my sin, just as I have to confess every hour that I do not love God and my neighbour perfectly.'

'Many earnest men disobey this commandment of the Holy Ghost, I am sure, because they feel the evil of their own hearts so strongly.'

'Now this is most absurd from a scriptural point of view. In fact, the very step on which a Christian plants his foot, and thence rises to true joy and true worship, is the total setting aside of his own evil nature, as so utterly worthless, unimprovable, and corrupt, that he determines, by God's help, he will have no confidence in it. If a man gets thoroughly into this scriptural truth about "the flesh," or rather, if it enters into him by the power of the Holy Ghost, he will soon rise into the higher experience of rejoicing in Christ Jesus, and then worshipping God in the Spirit.

'We shall try briefly to note the Scriptures that give us the history, character, and relations of this terrible foe, and from Scripture we shall find that man as man is no better and no worse than when he was driven out of Eden. Science and art have done much. Printing, railways, telegraphs, and many other inventions have appeared. Time and space, as to this little planet, have been almost annihilated. But what about real progress Godward? With all man's so-called improvements, are there fewer thieves? Has honesty risen much above the level of policy? Are servants more obedient to their masters? Are children more obedient to their parents? Development has been going on; but, alas! what development! The elements of all that has been developed were in Adam after the fall. Before the fall, Adam in innocence had body, soul, and spirit, with a will subject to God's will. By the fall he got, "the flesh,"—a self-will—a will independent of God's.'

Astronomers tell us that planets are kept in their courses by two forces acting in different directions, the resultant of which is the curve they describe round the sun. One of these forces would make the planet go *from* the sun, the other would draw the planet *to* the sun. The one force is centrifugal, the other is centripetal. Man revolving around God in the communion of innocence, having received the breath of life from God, making him immortal, and having been made in the image of God, acted as the representative of God on earth below. By the fall he severed his centripetal connection, or that which made him seek God, so that his action when he heard God's voice was to hide himself. He has now acquired this fatal self-will. A will which consults for self, and is not subject to the will of God. The fatal freedom is his that some planet let loose from its circular path would have; and now, in his mad, desolating, destructive, rebellious, God-dishonouring freedom, man, as man, is rushing on to everlasting chaos, confusion, and night, "the blackness of darkness for ever." The least thing could sever the link that joined man in probation to God. Disobedience to one test-act did it.

Man died (became separated... the
moment he ate the forbidden fruit...
been the history of the world ever...

Our modern sages tell us that it ha...
education of the world, that at Babel...
divided into classes, that under law man...
began in earnest, that Christ came as ...
great series of teachers, and now the Sp...
day is going on to complete the educat...
sounds very well, but it is only man's...
Scripture shows us that the history of t...
is the history of sin, that man is away ...
and must be (not educated, but) saved...
for ever. The ritualists tells us that m...
religionised; God tells us that he must ...
again. The rationalist tells us he has be...
on with his *education*; God tells us th...
'*condemned* already,' and is incapable ...
educated until His grace saves him. (T...

We have seen whence 'the flesh' was ...
let us look at it—

1. AS TRIED AND DESCRIBED BY GO...

There are two distinct though co...
questions :

First, What is the history of 'the flesh'...
Second, How is 'the flesh' described in Scr...

I may state here, that there is often co...
in men's mind concerning what 'the fl...
This partly arises from the word 'flesh' be...
in two quite different senses in Scripture,...
majority of cases in the New Testament t...

… 'flesh,' and 'fleshly,' have to do
… of the body, such as 'flesh and
… Christ came in the flesh,' which of
… the evil nature which is spoken of in
… of the word. There was an old
… made sin resident in the flesh of the
… this led men to practise tortures and
… very few ever have such a thought
… are about a hundred passages in
… has this first meaning. In the fifty
… which the word is used it refers to the
…, the alienated affections, the self-will
… away from God.

What is the history of the flesh?

… of arsenic in a glass full of water is
… the water, and cannot be detected by
… The chemist, in order to prove to the
… of all that it is deadly poison, takes
… and to it adds something else, which,
… it comes in contact with the arsenic in
…, makes it assume a well-known colour,
… at once what it is. He then takes another
… and adds something else to it to confirm
… by various tests he has shown us
… what it is, and proved beyond a doubt
… that poison. God has been doing this
…; not, as the rationalist would persuade
… to improve the arsenic, and make it a
… drink—arsenic remains arsenic. A far-
… a hundred acres of land, when trying
… manures and crops, does not require to
… land under one trial, but may have a

M

hundred distinct trials on his [...]
God did not try man twice in innocen[ce...]
not put two nations under law. Man [...]
as to nature being of the same materia[l...]
look at some of these tests that God [is]
employing from age to age.

1st, As an innocent man, God gave [a]
test—a thing which in itself had no mo[ral...]
He was allowed all the fruit in the gard[en]
that of one tree. The simplicity of the [test]
it all the more important. Man chose [his]
way; showed his independence—that is to [say]
as to his will. God knew what was in [man;]
was not for Himself He tried man. He [knew the]
end from the beginning; but that all mig[ht see]
it, and every mouth be stopped, man [...]

2d, After the fall man was tried as h[aving a]
will opposed to God, and a conscience [...]
of God's demands. Man had the knowl[edge]
of good and evil. His conscience told hi[m what]
he *ought* to do; he had no external laws t[o...]
'Leave a man to his conscience,' we hear [...]
We answer, 'He has been left,' and wh[at...]
see? That as the one test acting on [innocent]
man brought out his independence, o[r as]
to the will, so man, with the flesh in him[, and]
conscience, manifested his corruption or [deprav-]
ity of heart in lust, or sin as to the affecti[ons;]
we read, 'God *saw* that the wickedness [of man]
was great in the earth, and that *every* ima[gination]
(purposes and desires) of the thoughts of h[is heart]
was only evil continually.' Look at th[e]

... *in the Flesh.'* 179

... that is without exception, not one
... to the core; '*only*,' unadulterated
... sinfulness; '*continually*,' at every
... called good moments as well as
... a picture man, when he was left to
... thus presented! God alone saw
... in its innate hideousness; and so,
... had been thus tested for nearly two thou-
... till sin reached its height, God destroyed
... millions, in His wrath emptied
... destruction the earth odious in His
... a chemist hastens to throw out some
... compound made between a poison and a
... had God covenanting with Noah, and
... promise to Abraham, and His *law* to
... This brings us to the third test.
... law—the perfect rule of human right-
... given to one nation, as the test was
... to one man, and conscience had tried
... world (the whole Gentile world being
... guilty by conscience and the light of
... seen in Rom. i.) What did the law do?
... bring the nation to God? Here is what
... Ghost says, 'Wherefore then serveth the
... was added *for the sake of* (*lit.*) trans-
... (Gal. iii. 19.) What before was inde-
... that is, sin of the will, or corruption—
... of lust, was now seen to be transgres-
... is to say, sin in relation to law.
... law is, there is no transgression.'
... very well there was sin—so much that
... world had to be drowned; but law

showed sin to be transgression. A test, before it is of any use, must be perfect. If the test is imperfect, the results will prove nothing; but 'God's law is perfect,' it is 'holy, and just, and good;' and the moment it came in contact with 'the flesh'—with sinful man—it brought out his character as radically disobedient. Making the golden calf, and thus breaking the first words of the law, was man's reception of the law. The law was weak to make sinful men holy, weak not in itself, but weak through the flesh. Fouler and fouler the filthy water of the flesh is shown to be. Can anything be worse than independence (being away from God), corruption, and transgression? Yes, one thing more was needed before the trial of the flesh could be completed. Passing over man's declension under kings subject to God, and Gentile wickedness in unlimited monarchy over the whole world, we come to Christ as the last test at the 'end of the world' under trial.

4th, Christ is seen as a test of man. A servant might be very independent, or very corrupt, or break his master's commands, but he might never, with all this, have thought of taking his master's life. If the testing process had stopped short of Christ as a test, the nature of the flesh would not have been fully seen; but He has proved what man is. We are so much accustomed to think of Christ as a Saviour, that we seldom think of Him as coming to bring out 'what was in man.' Read Mark xii. 1-10. After showing man in his treatment of subordinate servants, the **Lord** says,

therefore one Son, His well-
... Him also *last* unto them saying,
... reverence My son."' We know well
... did; they slew the King's Son, show-
... their enmity to the King. Enmity
... God Himself is the highest point rebellion
... ! This was never seen till Christ came;
... the education of the world! Read
... 22-24, 'If I had not come and spoken
... they had not had sin, but now they
... cloke for their sin, He that hateth me
... my Father also. If I had not done among
... works which none other man did they
... had sin but now have they both seen and
... me and my Father.'

... recapitulate what we have seen to be
... character of man from his history. God
... him, and the very first thing recorded
... each test is evil.

... tried in innocence, his *independence*
... that is, sin as to the will.

... As tried by conscience, his *corruption* was
... that is, sin as to the heart.

... As tried by law, his *transgression* was
... that is, sin as to commandment.

... As tried by Christ, his *enmity* was seen—
... sin as to a person.

... complete character of the poison is now
... the flesh' would kill God if it could. Man
... flesh' slaughtered the God-man. Friend,
... that nature in your bosom.

... *How is the flesh described?*

How does God describe it in [the docu]ments of His word? It is remarkable [that] until the full proof had been given of wh[at it] can do—namely, crucify Christ—that [it was] spoken of and fully exposed by God, and [by] God its true character. The flesh is [not] borne with now on account of the har[dness of] men's hearts, for the darkness is past, [the] true light now shineth. In Rom. vii. [he] says, 'I know that in me (that is, in [my flesh,]) dwelleth no good thing.' This proves th[e presence] of two natures in the Christian, as [also] the fearfully depraved character of the fles[h. The] Holy Ghost dwelt in Paul as He dwells i[n the] Christian. But besides his new nature th[ere is] still the old, unchanged and unchangeable. [None] but a saved man can know that there is [no] *good* whatever in 'the flesh.' Many mo[st] converted men believe that there are ma[ny bad] things in it, but none of them believe tha[t there] is nothing good. 'Even the worst have good points' is man's estimate (and it i[s] true as to human morality); but God's e[stimate] is 'nothing good.' Read Gen. vi. 5. All [know] they are sinners, but few that they (a[s come] from Adam) are nothing but sinners. The [extent] of the ruin, the nature of the depravity, a[nd the] steps by which it was reached, are of co[mpar]atively little importance, since in every [un]verted man (as God sees him) there is no[good] thing.

A friend who had been led to see th[is]

■■■ labelled all *my* feelings with
■■■ good thing."' When a very
■■■ is converted, his friends often say,
■■■ he was a thoughtless young man and
■■■■, but he was not so bad as some
■■■ so on, with a great deal of palliation
■■■ sentimentalism, instead of affixing to
■■■ estimate of every unconverted man, 'No
■■■

■■■ people think, that because they under-
■■■ great deal of theological truth, that there-
■■■ have some germ of good within them.
■■■ man has been born again, all his know-
■■■ however good in itself, is reckoned 'no good
■■■ him.
■■■ think that because they feel devotional
■■■ sights and plaintive pealing pipes of
■■■ machinery, there must be some soft corner
■■■ things in their hearts after all; but God
■■■ says, '*no good thing.*' Hearing the
■■■ March in Saul' played by a military band
■■■ funeral has often moved many to
■■■ I do not wonder at the most stolid
■■■ moved in their feelings; but what does
■■■ ing or emotion amount to?—'*No good*
■■■

■■■ again suppose because their consciences
■■■ urbed at certain sins, that this is so much
■■■ Man has nothing to boast of in having a
■■■ not even if he follow its right leadings.
■■■ never gave a new nature. Every man
■■■ conscience, that is to say—the knowledge of

good and evil. A man cannot [...]
because he has a thermometer which [...]
it is warm. Neither has a man any[...]
because he has within him that which [...]
what is good, and what is evil. Let [...]
other Scriptures to find out a little more [...]
flesh is.

Gal. v. 19, 'The works of *the flesh* are [...]
which are, adultery, fornication, unclean[...]
civiousness, idolatry, witchcraft, hatred, [...]
emulations, wrath, strife, seditions, heresies, [...]
ings, murders, drunkenness, revellings, and [...]
like.' What a fountain of all uncleanness [...]
2 Pet. ii. 18 we find what feeds the flesh [...]
when they speak great swelling words of [...]
they allure through the lusts of *the flesh.* [...]
flesh loves pompousness, it hates humility [...]
Pet. ii. 10 speaks of 'them that walk after [...]
flesh in the lust of uncleanness, and [...]
government—presumptuous, self-willed.' [...]
will,' (that is, liking and choosing one's own [...]
rather than God's,) is, in fact, the very [...]
of the flesh.' Man must have what he will [...]
desires, whatever the consequences be, wh[...]
God says; Satan, of course, at the same [...]
blinding us as to what God's will is. The [...]
is also in close alliance with its lusts: 1 J[...]
16, 'All that is in the world, the lust of the [...]
and the lust of the eyes, and the pride of [...]
not of the Father but is of the world.'

Rom. viii. 3-7 gives us the nature of th[...]
as opposed to *law*, to *life*, and to *God*, just [...]

... history. Ver. 3, 'What ... do in that it was weak through ... 7, 'The carnal mind (literally the ...) is not subject to the *law* of God, ... can be.'. It opposed the law, broke ... up to more evil by it. Again, as ... 6, 'To be carnally minded (literally *... the flesh*) is *death*;' and as to God, ... mind is *enmity* against God;' ver. ... they that are in *the flesh* cannot ... Friend, pause a minute. Are you ...? Do what you may, you 'cannot ...' Give all your time and money to ... you 'cannot please God.' Let us ... 'the flesh'—

... AS TO THE SINNER'S SALVATION.

... not dwell long on this, as we have seen ... character of it is. 'The flesh' is never ... improved. It can only be con-... Christ came in the likeness of sinful flesh, ... condemned '*sin-in-the-flesh*.' 'The ... forgiven. It is judged, set aside, ... Though my sins were like scarlet, ... blood has cleansed them, and I am for-... the flesh never is. God never improves ... never forgives it, neither should we. ... ved from this awful depravity and ... in which we were born, not by any ... work, any more than we are justified ... by a work.

... of *the flesh* just as we got into it.

We got into it by our birth; we [get out by]
a new birth. We got into it in a [fallen]
head, Adam; we get out of it in the [risen]
head, Christ. Christ on the cross not [only]
our iniquities laid upon Him, but also [for]
'sin in *the flesh*;' that is to say, not [the]
sin, but sin in the nature; not the bra[nches,]
the root; not the streams, but the foun[tain.]

Many are trying to improve 'the [flesh.']
would take much comfort if they could [see]
themselves getting a little better; wh[ereas God]
wishes us to have no confidence in it [at all,]
and to 'reckon ourselves dead indeed [to sin.']
How could any one without a new natu[re change]
his flesh by any effort of will, since 'fles[h is]
self-will? It would only be will against [will, which]
is an absurdity.

But if I receive God's Christ as the [One who died]
and now risen, reckoning myself dead t[o sin, I]
bring in God's will done in Christ's wor[k for]
sin, and I thus 'thank God through Jesu[s Christ]
our Lord,' and begin to walk in newn[ess of life.]
And though there is still conflict, I kno[w that]
'with the mind I myself (what God reck[ons]
me in Christ) serve the law of God, but [with the]
flesh the law of sin;' but that 'there is [no con-]
demnation to them who are in Christ [Jesus.']
Whether are you in Christ Jesus or in th[e flesh?]
You cannot be in both.

Your standing is either in Christ ris[en or in]
Adam fallen. There is no third man. [Adam]
was the first man, and all the trial wa[s in him.]

...is the second man, and
... He is the last. He is the
... is the last Adam. (1 Cor. xv.

... TO THE CHRISTIAN'S LIFE.

...Scripture is very plain on two

...Christian is not in '*the flesh.*' Paul
...himself and of all Christians thus,
...in the flesh,' (Rom. vii. 5,) of
...ing that they were no longer in it.
...is still in the Christian. Paul
...that is in my flesh, dwelleth no good
...vii. 18.) If we mistake or forget
...these facts, we shall get into great
...shall have lessened power in dealing
...

...CHRISTIAN IS NOT IN THE FLESH.

...in the flesh but in the Spirit, if so
...of God dwell in you.' (Rom.
...Spirit of God dwells in all Christians,
...is true of all. 'They that are
...*crucified* the flesh with the affections
...(Gal. v. 24.) Not 'are to crucify,' or
...'*have crucified.*' 'In whom also
...with the circumcision made
...in putting off the body of the sins
...the circumcision of Christ.' (Col.
...Christian is out of Adam and in
...sailing now in the river of life,

whereas by nature his boat is tossing on the river of death. It is said of the children of Israel in the wilderness, so wicked and so perverse, God 'hath not beheld iniquity in Jacob, neither hath He seen perverseness in Israel.' (Num. xxiii. 21.) So when God looks at a sinner in Christ He sees the sinner dressed in all the beauty of Christ and sees none of the sinner's iniquity nor perverseness.

The Holy Spirit, by the pen of the Apostle Paul, brings out this very clearly in the second chapter of Galatians, where a line of argument is pursued similar to that contained in the sixth of Romans. In Romans, after Paul brings in 'all the world,' Jew and Gentile, 'guilty before God,' and demonstrates the victory of grace over sin, he goes on in the sixth chapter to shew Christ in resurrection, as the immediate and effective power of personal holiness.

In the second of Galatians he takes occasion from Peter's refusing to take a meal with certain persons, to shew the true position and standing of all believers in the Lord Jesus Christ. A straw shews the direction of the current. If Peter could not have intercourse with Gentiles who had been cleansed by the blood of Christ and placed in a position of righteousness that no legal observances could effect or help them to keep and walk in, the whole 'gospel of the grace of God' would be undermined. (Read Gal. ii.)

Paul shews that both Peter and himself, Jews as they were, children of the promise, and not 'sinners of the Gentiles,' had to fall into the sinner's place, and accept Christ the gift of God.

Peter, in Acts xv. 11, stands up for the very same doctrine:—'We believe that, through the grace of the Lord Jesus Christ, we (Jews) shall be saved, even as they (sinners of the Gentiles).'

Paul says in effect, if the law could justify them, they were doing wrong in preaching Christ. Does Christ need the law to help Him to present the believer to God? We consider it blasphemous to think that Christ would be a minister of sin. But having been judged, condemned, and slain by the law, do we now go back to be saved or helped by it? If so, we prove by this very act that we are 'transgressors;' for in that case we should never have left it at all. Grace and law cannot help each other in our salvation—the adoption of grace is the giving up of law for salvation.

The Apostle, in the 18th and following verses (Gal. ii.) regards himself as representing all believers, and goes on to shew that men can serve God, and live acceptably to Him, only through death and resurrection. 'For I through the law am dead or more literally " died."' This of course, cannot mean that I am morally dead to the knowledge of its demands, nor that I am dead in the sense of seeking my justification by the old dispensation under law; but 'I *through* the law have died,' or have judicially met my doom. God said, 'In the day that thou eatest thereof thou shalt surely .' The flaming sword that guarded Paradise demanded my blood. 'I have died.' 'The

soul that sinneth it shall die.'
The law has exacted its demand[s...]
of sin is death.' These wages have [been?]
have died.'

But since I through the law have [a per-]
fect righteousness and justice I am now [met?]
its every claim, and the sword cannot [bathe]
in blood twice for the same offence. T[he life]
of my sin cannot be demanded twice. [A mur-]
derer hanging dead on the gibbet of ju[stice is]
to every demand which law can bring a[gainst him.]

Daniel, by serving his God, had bro[ught him-]
self under the penalty of the laws of [the Medes]
and Persians, which said, 'He shall be [cast into]
the den of lions.' But, sitting at the [bottom of]
that den with the lions' mouths gracious[ly shut,]
he could say,—'I am dead to the law [of the]
Medes and Persians.' And when Dari[us sought]
him on the morrow, he did so in perfect r[ighteous-]
ness as far as the demands of the la[w of the]
Medes and Persians were concerned, and [no foe]
of Daniel, no adviser of Darius, could [accuse]
the prophet for law breaking, nor poin[t the sus-]
picious finger at him as he sat with D[arius. He]
could now live to Darius. 'I through the [law am]
dead to the law,' only however, 'that I m[ight live]
unto God.'—'He that has died is justi[fied from]
sin.' (Rom. vi. 7.) This death and res[urrection]
scheme is no figure of speech, but an aw[ful fact]
as seen at Calvary, and a reality (judicia[lly and]
experimentally) to the sinner on believi[ng on the]
Lord Jesus Christ. We have life out of [death,]

...) explains the 18th.
... expresses the truth ab-
... meets this question,—'What!
... Saul the persecutor, Saul the
... legalist, dead?' He is; but
... finds an end of himself—on the
... 'I am crucified with Christ.' This
... obtained, 'as Christ was crucified
... the hands of the world, so I'll bear
... with Him.' It is indeed a blessed
... have fellowship with Him in His
... righteousness, and that as followers
... Jesus, we are to take up *our* cross
... ; but the truth in this passage
... statement in the former verse, 'I
... have died;' and to that in Ro-
... knowing that our old man is (has
... .' 'I have been crucified with
... verb is in the perfect passive). The
... against me fell on Him. My cup
... Him; my wages of sin were paid
... my separation from God was in His
... my God, why hast thou forsaken
... was borne by Him—the perfectly
... fulfilling all law, and then bearing
... me the unrighteous, condemned,
... suffered, the Just for the unjust,
... bring us to God.' 'He hath
... be sin for us who knew no sin, that
... made the righteousness of God in
... back on His cross, and identi-
... with Him, I can say—

> '*I through the law am d[ead],*'
> '*I am crucified with Ch[rist.]*'

No demand can be made against [him:]
after justice had been appeased, God ra[ised]
up from the dead by the Holy Spirit,
there could never come one single que[stion con-]
cerning sin against Him who had become [sin-]
bearer (after having borne sin, He was [raised in]
righteousness), so I quickened into this [newness]
of life,' go free. He was raised again for [jus-]
tification, and on believing I reckon mys[elf dead,]
and can say—

> '*I am dead to the law,*'
> '*Crucified; nevertheless I live*'—

live in Christ raised from the dead, uni[ted to]
Christ beyond His grave, beyond the dem[ands of]
law, beyond the doom of sin, for it is [not I]
(literally *no longer*) I, but Christ liveth i[n me—]
no longer Saul the Pharisee—Saul the p[retender]
to and striver after righteousness by law, [but one]
who has submitted himself to God's righ[teousness]
—one who has submitted himself to be p[ut out of]
existence judicially, that is to say, in God's [reckon-]
ing—and is now known only as one who [is alive]
in Christ, living unto God—

> '*That I might live unto God;*'
> '*Yet not I, but Christ liveth in m[e.]*'

A man is thus made fit for living unto [God, not]
by amendment and reformation, but [by]
death and *resurrection:* the flesh atte[mpts the]
former, in the latter God alone can wo[rk.]

.... I live in a foreign
.... I have no friends, no
.... faith,' on what will be
.... of God.' This life feeds
.... in Christ, 'who loved me
.........'

.... only forgiveness of sins in
.... also; for I could no more
.... law, than I could forgiveness.
.... the righteousness of God in
.... come by law, Christ
........., but we are in Him 'who of God
.... wisdom, and righteousness, and
.... and redemption.' (1 Cor. i. 30.)
.... Christ we died to sin—
.... buried in His tomb;
.... now with Him our life,
.... beyond our doom.'

.... Paul places the believer in per-
.... before God, Christ his title, Christ
........., Christ his meetness, Christ his
.... partaker of the divine nature,' the
.... enjoy God and commune with

.... all this truth to do with the Chris-
.... life, one may ask? Much, very
.... for there can be no real progress
.... in the Christian course until the
.... standing before God be righteously
.... settled.

.... of Adam, of the will of the flesh,
.... Adam's nature, its guilt, its actings

N

and its doom, 'by nature the [children of wrath].' So having received Christ, [being born of God] we are reckoned as one with Christ, [as having been] crucified with Christ, and thus [having died to] sin in Christ: and now we live, to [God, the] life of Christ, a life in resurrection; [thus] getting a new nature at the second [birth as we] got the Adam nature at the first. [God reckons] us as being thus in His sight; and we [believing] and thus getting into God's reckoning, [to us] there is 'no condemnation to them [in] Christ Jesus.'

2d. THE FLESH IS IN THE CHRISTIAN.

No Christian ever lived or ever will [live on] earth, without sin in him. Indeed it [is as I] know Christ that I really know the utter [worth-] lessness of the flesh, that 'in me (that [is in my] flesh) dwelleth no good thing.' (Rom. [7.]) Now, the opposition will be felt between [the] perfectly holy nature, begotten in me in [union] with Christ risen and gone to the Father, [and the] perfectly sinful nature. Now it is that [I see] the meaning of 'sin that *dwelleth* in [me.' It] can never be uprooted here for it *dwelleth*. This is something different from sins com[mitted in] me, committed by me, or felt by me. [I] realize what sin is, the innate princip[le of my] nature, the root of all my sins, which [I now] find is not merely the cause of occa[sional sins,] and is no accident or habit, but 'sin d[welleth in] me.' Formerly I might have assum[ed]

... sin was true, but now I ... 18), that is, the truth is ... conscience by the Holy Ghost. ... the disposition of the flesh (lit.) ... God, for it is not subject to the ... neither indeed can be.' (Rom. viii. 7.) ... above it will be seen that salvation ... more than a mere payment of debt, ... over of iniquity, the gift of a white ... righteousness, a setting right of the ... the soul, for which, out of gratitude ... aided by His Spirit, the Christian is ... a holy life. There is also a new ... implantation of a nature which not ... a man live to serve God out of ... but which in its very essence is *from* ... over the spring of all true Christian ... the presence and operative power of ... Spirit, working indeed through a ... faculties, but on objects above and ... the Adam-life can see, apprehend, ... enjoy. Three very important and prac... ... arise out of the foregoing truths.

... Christian has two natures in one per-

... Christian grows in grace: How?
... Christian daily confesses his sins, and ... given.

... Christian has two distinct natures in one responsible person.

... is not two persons, the one perfectly sinful, and the other perfectly [holy, shut] up together in one chamber; [but the two] natures, the 'old' and the 'new man' [in the] responsible person; he has that born [of the flesh] which is not merely flesh-like but *flesh*, [and that] born of the Spirit which is not merely [spirit-like] but *spirit*.

The sinner once living 'in the flesh,' ['dead in] trespasses and sins,' is now pardoned, [saved,] and made a saint—Christ having died [and risen] for him—by being born again, in reality [and] in figure begotten by the Holy Ghost. As [such] he is now 'not in the flesh,' though [the flesh is] in him, but he is in the Spirit, and is [responsible] for the uprisings and sins of the old [man, but] is henceforth pardoned as a son, according [to the] value of the blood presented before God [for him;] the person, the individual, now become a [Chris-]tian, the man possessed of these two natures, should be walking 'in the spirit,' though [ever] and anon he is made to stumble through [the] power of the 'flesh.' Thus the saint does [not] advance in sanctification, by a change [being] effected in the character of either nature, [but by] the gradual development of 'the new man' [by] means of the inworking of the Holy Ghost, [and] in the daily mortification of the members [which] are upon the earth. The man is thus [gradually] sanctified and made more like Christ. [This is] growth 'in grace.' How blessed! We are [saved] 'by *grace*;' we stand 'in *grace*'—we grow [in *grace*.'] The life of a child is perfectly [happy.]

... man. The smallest leaflet
... of the vine has the same
... branch, the trunk or the
... implanted is a perfect life: we
... up to the stature of men. We
... up briefly regarding this new
... we have already discoursed on at
... chapter on the work of the Spirit.
... we get the origin and communica-
... 'Ye must be born again' (ver. 7):
... all of God, must be implanted;
... already in me wrought on and
... water and of the spirit' the word
... by the Spirit purifies us as to our
... and affections.
... we get the indwelling of the
... of Christ—as the one energizing
... new man, represented as 'a well of
... up into everlasting life.' (iv. 14.)
... we get the outflow of this Spirit,
... of the new man on all around
... no new channels, no new faculties
... 'out of his belly shall flow rivers
...' (ver. 38.)

... *grows in grace: How? Does*
... old heart get better?

... Gospel the Spirit of God teaches that
... man there is a new fountain.
... Christians seem to think that all we get
... is a divinely given *filter* to the old
... will gradually increase in its

power until it renders the filthy water of the fountain clean. In Galatians v. the whole point is stated. Two *fountains* are spoken of in the converted man, sending out two natural streams. The streams from one fountain, the flesh, are given at the 19th: 'Adultery, fornication, uncleanness, lasciviousness, idolatry, witchcraft, hatred, variance, emulations, wrath, strife, seditions, heresies, envyings, murders, drunkenness, revellings.' Are we anywhere told in Scripture that this evil nature is really purified? Certainly, indeed, the man, the individual, is purified, is cleansed, is made holy, is morally sanctified; but it is in altogether another way than by trying to cure the 'incurably wicked.' The streams from the other fountain—the Spirit—are given at the 22nd: 'love, joy, peace, long-suffering, gentleness, goodness, faith, meekness, temperance;' and we are told that the Christian's holy life is walking in the Spirit, mortifying the 'members which are upon the earth' (Col. iii. 5), keeping them in their place of death, 'not fulfilling the lust of the flesh.' This is God's way; He asks for a holy walk, and moreover He has not left us powerless, as helpless slaves under the flesh; He has placed us in a position above it, as masters over it—for 'the flesh lusteth against the Spirit, and also the 'Spirit against the flesh, and these are contrary the one to the other' (therefore can never be merged the one in the other, or come to peaceable terms) '*in order that*

... things that ye would.' Not, ... stood, that I wish to do good ... not (we get that aspect of truth in ... quickened man under law in Rom. ... is another thought here); but on ... that while by the flesh-nature I ... evil things, I have now the Spirit in- ... acting, restraining me from doing ... which I naturally would do. ... Christians do not know that we become ... at the new birth; hence they do ... the existence in the believer of two ... opposite and actively opposing ... ignorance of these things is at the root ... confounding errors in doctrine and

... consisted merely in having forgive- ... powers of the mind being set right, and ... wrought on and sanctified, we might be ... and lost to-morrow; in Christ to- ... of Him to-morrow. But if I get a ... the child's life, being 'quickened ... with Christ,' united to Christ by the ... sent down from heaven—I am as ... saved as Christ is safe, for I am a ... of His body, of His flesh, and of His ... (Eph. v. 30.)

... if my sinful propensities had merely to ... down, so that they should gradually die ... one, until all of them should cease to ... if I were to live long enough, and ... ently zealous, watchful, and prayerful

I might obtain perfection in its [...] moral sense,—might live without [sin at] all. This we know is opposed to [all] teaching, for (it is written of Christ[ians]) say that we have no sin, we deceive our[selves,] the truth is not in us.' It is equally op[posed to] all conscientious Christian experience, [for though] we *ought* at all times to walk 'in the Spir[it' with-] out sinning, we know that the unch[angeable,] unchangeable root of sin remains till we [...]. That kind of teaching which speaks of the [attain-]ment of perfection in the walk of a Chri[stian,] that is to say, the possibility of sinless p[erfection,] perfect sanctification in the flesh, tends n[ot only] to tone down sin, and make it a light mat[ter, but] sacrilegiously brings down God's standard [of holi-]ness to human attainment, instead of hav[ing it] in Christ: Christ *for me*—my Substitute; [Christ] *in me*—my life.

In 1 John iii. 9. we read, 'Whosoever [is born] of God doth not commit sin; for His seed [remain-]eth in him, and he cannot sin, because he [is born] of God.' Mark very carefully that this [is not] written concerning a few advanced Christ[ians who] had reached a high state of perfection, [but is] written concerning the youngest disciple[s: 'Who-]soever is born of God.' And would it [not be] strange to think that anything born of God [could] sin? The difficulty in the passage vanishe[s when] I understand that the Christian has two n[atures,] one born of God, perfect and sinless (God['s seed] is in him), the other born of Adam, imp[erfect] sinful. Whenever a Christian commits a sin, he is not manifesting that he is born of God, but is showing that he is born of Adam. It is not as born of God he sins, but as born of Adam. Should we not watch over ourselves, and pray for much grace, to enable us always to live as sons of God, and not as sons of Adam? The practical holiness of a believer is not attained by an act as his justification is. The Spirit compares it to *fruit* growing, increasing and ripening, till God and the believer shall be satisfied with it when Christ shall appear and we shall all be like Him. Blessed be God this is our calling. We are to be holy as God is holy. We shall be satisfied when we awake in His likeness, and never till then.

It is Christians who are told, in Phil. iii. 3. to have no 'confidence in the flesh.' Those who are the true circumcision of God have no confidence in any religious culture, advantages, or natural privileges. Paul could boast more than any man of natural trainings for the flesh. Born under and brought up in all God's ordinances, he yet had to renounce all. God's ordinance can never implant life. All our many privileges could never implant the new life. They can, and do develope the life, as the heat, sunshine, rain, and culture do a seed; but an act of God's Spirit is required to implant the seed. These same privileges may only the more surely seal the ruin of a man who has not been converted, and it may be impossible to renew him to repentance. The sun hardens the clay as it softens wax. Paul thought all his natural ad-

...vantages but loss. He had no [...] flesh. Two are striving for the [mastery in a] Christian, the flesh and the spirit—['the flesh] lusts against the Spirit, and the Sp[irit against the] flesh.' But we have now the upper [hand. Sin] shall not have dominion over us. [It may war,] but shall not reign over us. It is b[y conflict] and warfare, not by assimilation and [compromise,] that we grow in the Christian life. [We are] daily sanctified by the 'flesh' getting [weaker and] less, by the new nature in us growing [and being] strengthened by the indwelling Spirit [of God,] thus successfully opposing the first na[ture, the] flesh. We cannot expel the flesh—[we must hold it] dead, put it off, and keep it under. [We must mortify] our members which are upon the ear[th. We] cannot root out the vile weeds—we [must keep the] scythe going cutting them down.

All Christians would wish to be [led by the] Spirit: but they forget the first step, t[o give] a vote of '*no confidence*' in the flesh. [As a] subsequent step there will then be wat[ching as] well as looking to Christ, who is our [life.] The Christian has not so much to fear [the flesh] in its outwardly gross forms, as in its th[ousand] desires. It is comparatively easy no[t] to tell lies, not to swear, not to be a dr[unkard.]

Many moral, unconverted men are [capable] of the highest external right-doing; but [it is in its] secret workings, workings that are nat[ural,] that we have most to dread the flesh.

Our path is that of obedience and h[oliness...]

footsteps of our Lord, where the righteous requirements of the law are 'fulfilled in us, who walk not after *the flesh*, but after the Spirit,' (Rom. viii. 4), for the flesh gave us nothing in the past, and can profit us nothing for the future: thus 'we are debtors not to the flesh, to live after the flesh.' For 'if ye live after the flesh, ye shall die; but if ye through the Spirit do mortify the deeds of the body, ye shall live.' (Rom viii. 12, 13.) Our sonship cannot be taken from us, but we can have no living fellowship with God if we thus walk. 'Living after the flesh' and communion with God cannot possibly go together. Death is separation from God—not 'ceasing to exist;' for we know that not even the lost thus perish. Death is ceasing to exist in one state or condition, and existing in another state separated from God.

Take care, fellow-disciple, of getting into a deadened state of soul. We have the flesh in us, yet we have no authority, but the reverse, for living after it, 'as if we walked according to the flesh.' (2 Cor. x. 2.) Stamp upon it 'no confidence'—'Put ye on the Lord Jesus Christ, and make not provision for the flesh, to fulfil the lusts thereof.' (Rom xiii. 14.) Alas! how often we make provision for it! How the flesh feasts upon praise and flattery! It likes to be flattered, and when it is not flattered, it begins to flatter. It understands nothing about being of 'no reputation.' It likes to be something, or to do something. 'Though I be nothing' is not in its vocabulary. Have I done something for the Lord? Have I been the poor humble channel to convey water to a soul? The flesh likes to know it. 'Let not thy left hand know what thy right hand doeth'—is God's way. 'Let not only your left hand, but let every person know'—is man's way. 'I did so and so. I was used in so and so.' Oh, this fearful self! This awful I! And then it, of course, vindicates itself. 'Oh, but it is for God's glory that I tell it!' Yes; this may be the worst part of the whole—taking a little to self under semblance of giving all to God. 'No provision,' 'no confidence' in your own evil nature, or any other person's. Take care of being 'vainly puffed up' by the mind of the flesh. (Col. ii. 18.) Do not be unkind to a fellow-believer by bringing near him that which the flesh enjoys. Do not bring sparks near gunpowder. 'Oh, you did well to-day!' said one to another who had preached the gospel. 'Yes,' he replied, 'Satan told me that before I left the pulpit.' Let us not serve Satan after this sort.

None are in greater danger than those who are used to gather in souls. I knew one who was constantly used of God in doing all kinds of good, and when he did speak, it was always about what other people had been doing. To tell his faults to a friend himself is faithfulness. All that is good of him tell to others. God tells us of our faults. He stands up for us against every accuser. Another I knew who could speak of what self had been used in doing, but could not bear to hear of others being used. What a God-dishonouring, flesh-gratifying as well as foolish course! Are we not members one of another? I heard it said of a dear Christian one day, 'Yes, such a one lives upon praise.' Do you live upon the rejected Lord, who made Himself of no reputation, or on praise? Husks that the swine live upon! Make no provision for the flesh.

'Having, therefore, these promises (the Lord Almighty to be our Father), dearly beloved, let us cleanse ourselves from all filthiness of *the flesh* and spirit, perfecting holiness in the fear of God.' (2 Cor. vii. 1.) You cannot be growing in grace, advancing in holiness, in these providings for the flesh. While the grace of God is not to be blamed for a moment, let us remember that we are under the righteous government of the Father, and 'he that soweth to his flesh shall of the flesh reap corruption.' Christians suffer, and suffer sadly, by sowing to, or making provision for, the flesh. Our only safeguard is Christ. With our eye steadfastly and constantly fixed on Him—following Him, copying Him, filled with Him—we shall be led into holiness of life, and neither into licentiousness nor into legalism. For while at the one extreme we may be led into licentiousness or carelessness of walk by our subtle foes, we have also to guard against another danger, which is asceticism and penance, a dishonour to the body by coming under worldly ordinances 'touch not, taste not, handle not,' which look very like holiness and consecration to God in neglecting our bodies, but in effect only tend 'to the satisfying of the flesh.' (Col. ii. 20.) For the flesh feasts on whatever is against Christ, and is satisfied with whatever takes the eye from Him.

'But will not the Holy Spirit keep His own from all this?' I have been asked. 'Yes; but the way He does keep us from the power of the flesh is by enabling us to give it no food, no provision, no satisfaction.' Whatever feeds the spirit starves the flesh. So the apostle Peter by the Holy Ghost says, 'Dearly beloved, I beseech you as strangers and pilgrims, abstain from fleshly lusts which war against the soul.' (1 Pet. ii. 11.) The ways of men around are strange ways to us. They think this advice is far above human reach (and so it is), but we are living the life of Christ; and as such, we are to hate, 'even the garment spotted by the flesh.' (Jude 23.) Alas! how little watching and praying there is among Christians—how little we live on Christ! If we lived with Him ever before us, ever filling us, our only satisfaction, our joy for ever, what power should we gain over 'the flesh!'

Christians learn what the 'flesh' is—

1st, By experience of its unmingled vileness before conversion; or its horrid lusts and sad sins after conversion; or

2d, By taking God's character of it from His Word.

When God gives us His 'Memoirs of olden times,' He does not leave out the actings of the flesh. When the 'chronicles of the spirits of just men made perfect' pass before us in Heb. xi., their sins and iniquities are remembered no more.

I have been much struck with the unreal life people are led into by reading memoirs of good people, where the good in their lives is told but not the evil, where the triumph is seen but not the conflict. It is just like 'novel literature,' that gives such unreal ideas to young people, and unfits them for everyday life. So most memoirs, by not bringing prominently forward the everyday conflicts, the evil foe within, often do more real harm than permanent good. Read God's own histories. Many human ones would do for angels or seraphs to read, but they are not for militant saints. 'Follow me,' says the Perfect One, and the Lord Jesus Christ is enough.

Dear worker-for-God, 'let no man take thy crown.' Take care of this foe. A brother in the Lord used to say often to himself, before going to do anything for God, as preaching, &c., 'Now, soul, honour bright, is this for the glory of God?' We need a great deal more of bright sterling honour between God and our souls, and also between one another. We fear the flesh most from its gradual uprisings. It has begun to work often before we are aware, and not till some text meets us straight in the face do we discover that the flesh has been working. Again, our religionised and pious flesh is often a great snare; that is to say, we sometimes begin to think that a Christian's 'flesh' is better than an unconverted man's 'flesh;' but, if we do, we proceed on false

grounds, and will reap not[hing...]
look to Christ away from your[...]
heart, live in the Spirit, and k[eep...]
Lord Jesus until you see Him as H[e is]
you shall be like Him, done with [...]
this corrupt nature, this self-willed fl[esh]
time we have to be daily, hourly con[...]
and in this having the most blessed [...]
with God—'in light' that makes [...]
manifest and overlooks nothing.

3. *The Christian daily confesses h[is ...]*
daily forgiven.

A perfect statement of the whole p[osition]
and restoration of a Christian is foun[d in]
i. If we are to have fellowship with [...]
and the Son, we must have that life i[...]
us by the Holy Ghost,—that eternal, [...]
perfect life, which is capable of havin[g ...]
with God—that nature which throbs [...]
with God's nature, for we are 'parta[kers of]
Divine nature.' (2 Pet. i. 4.)

We are *now* sons. Our place is n[ow in]
light and in the Spirit, and thus in [...]
if we were walking in darkness, in unl[...]
it would be merely *saying* we have [...]
and not the truth. God is now reveal[ed with-]
out a veil, and, wondrous truth! we [...]
walk 'IN THE LIGHT as God is in the [light]
the exercise of that pure and perfect [...]
[p]erfect commandment) that this whole [...]
[inc]ulcating (1 John ii. 9), following [...]

... the vilest confessed ... Pharisees, 'Neither do ... sin no more.' He was ... and becomes to all such ... His feet, the '*light of life.*' ... 'we have fellowship with ... having communion and ... God. Here shall we be able ... sins; in this very place, not ... 'the light,' but 'in the light' ... Christ His Son cleanseth *us* ... who have been born again) ... The blood is once applied and is ... — not has cleansed or did ... us from all sin.' The ... not to make us believe or feel ... no sin in us. Sin will be in every ... saint, till he goes hence; for 'If ... have no sin, we deceive ourselves, ... is not in us.' And what am I to ... sins that are still uprising, and ... makes manifest, for the more ... a room the more the dust is seen? ... simple plan!

... our sins, He is faithful and just ... our sins, and to cleanse us from all ... Confess our *sins*, not our *sin*, ... 'We are all sinners: God be ... a sinner;' but judging the up... evil spring, according to God's ... holiness, which is Christ, con... sins, deeds, looks, thoughts

o

What heart-searching this [implies,]
'[confess] our sins,' not merely in [word, but]
a real individual dealing with [God,]
as condemned sinners before an [angry God,]
all the more real, because we are [now]
dealing with such a holy, gracious [One,]
saying our wills were not in the [sins.]

'He is faithful and just.' It is [not a]
matter of love and mercy,—these [have]
provided the way: but He is 'faithful,' [He]
hath said it, He is 'just,' on account of [the blood]
presented there, 'to forgive,' and it is [our]
unbelief not to 'confess,' confide, and [believe]
we are forgiven on the spot, and [then are]
walking in the light with a calm, holy [joy.]

The first two verses of the second [give]
the apostle's practical interpretation of [the doc-]
trines. 'My little children, these [things write I]
unto you, that ye *sin not*.' No lower [standard is]
set before us than absolutely 'sin not,' [be ye]
holy, for I am holy.' (1 Pet. i. 15.) [Walk in the]
Spirit,' in the energy of the new life, [the new]
light; mortifying the deeds of the [body.]
This is certainly our aim, but in this [we are aim-]
ing yet not attaining.

But 'if any man sin, we have an [advocate]
(literally a paraclete, the same word [which is trans-]
lated 'Comforter' whom Christ was [to send, our]
friend here with us, being the Holy [Ghost; our]
friend on high is the Lord Jesus—our [advocate]
with the Father, Jesus Christ *the Right[eous],*
[H]e is the propitiation for our sins;

... the whole world.' That is
... Christians commit any sin as
... His character of advocate He
... it. This is very blessed, for
... confess all known sins and thus
... consciences, there are many sins
... see; but He has made Himself
... cleanse us from all sin which His
... And He is a righteous advocate,
... can by no means clear the guilty,
... wisdom! wondrous truth! won-
... He took our guilt upon Him, and
... His own death as that which
... all sin. He sees the sin—He
... Father—He is the advocate. He
... accuser—He is the propitiation. What
... paraclete with the Father our High
... God, ever keeping us clean by His
... Him; as the paraclete, the Holy
... He sent, is ever keeping us clean
... the Word, washing the feet of those
... every whit' (John xiii.), removing
... consciences every thing that *He sees*
... our fellowship and communion,
... which He whispers to us! (Eph. v. 26.)
... BROTHER,—You have died and
... Christ.' Is your affection set on those
... are above?' Do you think you
... God's mind concerning your stand-
... acceptance? Blessed, most blessed, if
... But does this lead you to be more
... Christ-like, more heavenly-minded,

more anxious to walk in [...] as a Christian, am 'not under [the law,' (Rom. vi. 14.) I am certainly under my Lord's [command-]ments. 'If ye love Me keep my [commandments.]' (John xiv. 15.) 'For this is the love [of God,] that we keep His commandments; [and His com-]mandments are not grievous.' (1 John [v. 3.])

'And this is His commandment, [that we] believe on the name of His Son Jesus [Christ,] (having believed—having the new [life), love one] another, as He gave us commandment.' [(1 John] iii. 23.) If we read all the practical [exhortations] at the end of Romans, Ephesians, Colo[ssians, etc.,] we shall find that Christians had to be [over and] again reminded whose they were, [and how they] ought to walk.

Two truths have to be kept in [mind: the] Christian is not under the law-princip[le—of his] being exacted for so much—the [task-master's] whip held over his head, with its '[do this and] live' demands—but he is quickened [by a life] received from God, in subjection to [Him, and] 'enlawed to Christ.' (1 Cor. ix. 21); [and then] in this wilderness, he is only too glad [for ex-]plicit directions concerning the minut[iæ of life] as well as its higher outlines; glad, [amid con-]fusion here, to know in what direction [his Father's] finger points, so that with all his soul [he may] judge his own sinful flesh, and walk w[here his] Father directs. Thus, in a very blessed [sense, the] son delights in the law (the *torah*, [or divine] 'finger-point') of his Father; he m[editates]

… in the Flesh.'   213

… Are you loving to be
… of God along the platform of
… which is based on His infinite
… against a mere doctrinal or in-
… of truth. Without the living
… puffeth up.' Beware of the
… swamps of a hateful antinomianism,
… the flesh, so common all around us in
… so apt to lurk in every heart. To
… is given of him shall much be re-
… have been made sons of such a
… in that blessed, holy, separated walk,
… eternal union with His own beloved
… not walk like sons?
… of myself crucified with Christ,
… existence, as it were, in the crucifixion
… and now identified with the living,
… not mysticism, but one of God's
… realities—foolishness, indeed, to
… wise—a mystery, revealed by the
… only to those who, self-emptied and
… as little children. When you be-
… Lord Jesus Christ did you not leave
… in His grave (in God's reckoning)?
… sunk into the depths of the sea, to
… no more? Were you crucified
… Then you have left the world also
… of Christ: the cross as truly stands
… Christian and 'the world,' as between
… and his sins. 'One with Christ'
… with the Father, makes you one
… His rejection by the world. The

former you have by faith, the [...] consequence from the exhibited life of [...]

Do you see yourself at the cross, [for] your trespasses? That blessed voice [that] quitted you says, 'Go, and sin no more'; you see yourself at the cross, 'justified [in all] things,' and set down in perfect right[eousness] before God? Know, dear brother, that [you are] to justify your own profession of faith before [men] by the good works of faith which they can [under]stand and appreciate; and also you [are to] justify, before men, that God who [has] acquitted you and set you down before [Him] in His own righteousness which is Christ [...]

Do you see yourself as one set apart [by] blood which has been taken from the [...] 'the holiest of all,' and reckoned by God [as one] whose 'life is hid with Christ in God'? [Know,] dear brother, that you are to be purify[ing your]self, even as He is pure. Having His [...] life and righteousness inside the veil, we [have the] high privilege to take His place of testim[ony and] rejection outside the camp. In the la[nguage of] faith, and regarding myself as God reck[ons me] once crucified, but now alive in Christ, [I] can say—

> 'So nigh, so very nigh to God,
> I cannot nearer be;
> For in the person of His Son,
> I am as near as He.'

And the necessary consequence of know[ing it] and living in the power of it, will be [...]

my prayer and cry,
... clogged soul, as I pant
... will ever be—

... Lord, my God,
... with Thee;
... fully Him I know,
... my joy shall be;
... like a ransomed child,
... Himself I see.'

... knowing that our 'citizenship
... iii. 20), with the risen Christ
... walk here as our example,
... ward, and homeward—living
... the devil, and the flesh—'strong
... is in Christ Jesus,' having the
... our strength?'
... Are you trying to perfect in
... has been begun in the Spirit?
... small matter that Christ has
... that you are now in Him?
... have? You are conscientiously
... ness; but still you are constantly
... much more about the old
... Christ for you and in you. Why
... are not reckoning as God has
... this useless warfare. There
... the fight of faith, the fight I
... against God's foes and mine, the
... and the flesh. This is 'a good
... also a most ignoble and Christ-
... a fight by which I try to make
... to purify the filthy fountain, to

wash the rags of the prodigal [...] the best robe—a living, perfect [...] 'The just shall LIVE by faith,' as well [...] ten by faith. Remember that [...] holy walk with God unless I know [...] made me a son.

God is well pleased with Christ, [...] not well pleased with Him!

'Ah!' you say, 'I am satisfied with [...] not with myself.'

Will you ever be pleased with [...] Would it be well for you if you were [...] then, at once, by faith, adopt Paul's [...] 'No longer I, but Christ.'—Christ [...] Whether it were Paul or Peter, he had [...] into the poor Gentile sinner's place, and [...] am a sinner, therefore, Christ for me.'

'But I am not a great sinner,' you [...]
He died for all kinds of sinners.

'But I am too great a sinner,' do you [...]
Do you deserve to be nailed to a cross [...] cursed thing? How far did the Lord Jesus [...] to reach your case? Are there any steps [...] lead from your position to His? He was [...] curse for us; He lay in the tomb, and you [...] in trespasses and sins'—are lying in [...] Has He not come down to the very spot [...] you are? Are there any stepping-stones [...] between two, who are both lying side [...] the place of death? Ah, no; the gospel [...] —The Saviour for the sinner! Christ [...] God's way of life for my way of death [...]

'... in the Flesh.'   217

... even to the grave, and became
... me. I believe in Him, and, as
... I leap at one bound straight out of
... to His throne. 'I am crucified
... nevertheless I live; yet not I, but
... in me.' This is not a matter
... all a matter of faith, merely appre-
... grace of God, 'I live by the faith of
... God, who loved me and gave Himself
... ii. 20.)
... you lose faith in man's creed—'I
... and have faith in God's.—'Christ for
... 'born again,' you are 'crucified with
... are now living in His risen life.
*... confidence in the flesh,' and then you
... in Christ Jesus, and worship God in*

... we *died* to sin,	Rom. vi. 8.
... in His tomb;	Rom. vi. 4.
... now with Him, our Life,	Eph. ii. 5.
... beyond our doom!	Rom. vi. 7.
... wondrous love,	Eph. ii. 4.
... us who were dead;	Eph. ii. 6.
... heavenlies, *made us sit*	Eph. ii. 6.
... our living Head.	Eph. i. 22.
... now appears	Heb. ix. 24.
... veil above;	Heb. vi. 19.
... complete in Him,	Eph. i. 6.
... in His love.	Rom. viii. 39.
... we now are made	1 Co. i. 30.
... ousness of God;	2 Co. v. 21.
... God, and *heirs* with Christ,	1 Jo. iii. 1.
... where He trod.	Col. iii. 1.

Rejected and despised,	Is. liii. 3.
He bore the open shame;	Heb. xii. 2.
As *fellow-sufferers*, journeying home,	Rom. viii. 17.
We glory in His name.	Acts v. 41.
Soon will the Bridegroom come,	Rev. xxii. 20.
His Bride from earth to call!	1 Thes. iv. 16.
We, *glorified* with Him, shall reign,	Rev. xx. 4.
Till God be all in all.	1 Co. xv. 28.

The Devil.

OUR ADVERSARY.

'I DO not believe in eternal punishment,' said a man one day to a friend of mine. 'But that does not alter the fact,' replied my friend. This remark led to the man's conversion. Is it wise to shut the eye to danger? We know best how to deal with a foe when we know all about him, his plans, his tactics.

Wellington became the greatest conqueror by knowing his enemies, their strength, and their stratagems. He is the skilled surgeon who has thought over all possible dangers that may arise, and is prepared to meet them. When the builder of the Menai Bridge was suggesting various cautions, his coadjutors sometimes said to him that he was raising difficulties. 'No,' he answered, 'I'm solving them.' And so for every accident he was prepared.

In our spiritual conflict it is folly to despise the strength of our foes, it is wisdom to reckon on a power infinitely stronger. Many in the present day do not believe that there is a devil. They do not feel or realize any workings on their consciousness as of an external power. They think, therefore, that the devil is merely a word of theologians, an expression that may be used to and frighten children, but that intelligent[?] this nineteenth century are not to be [taken by?] it. With their friends of old they say [he?] is neither angel nor spirit.' (Acts xxiii.[?]) this does not alter the fact that there [is one.] Men may conscientiously, and therefore [sincerely] believe a lie. In fact we find in 2 Th[ess.] that because men 'received not the love [of truth] that they might be saved, for this cause [God will] send them strong delusions that they should [believe] a lie, that they all might be damned who [believed] not the truth but had pleasure in unright[eousness.]

Others who believe from the teaching [of scrip-]ture, that there is a devil, have little [idea] of his personality. They do not see [or know?] that he is as truly a person, though [not as?] the Son of God his great opponent. [They think?] of Satan as a mere influence or power, [telling?] us that they have devil enough [when they?] have their own evil heart. And true [it is the heart is] 'deceitful above all things and incura[bly wicked.]' But that Satan is a present, scheming, [artful,] cunning being, going about seeking [destruc-]tion, is realised by few; and by tho[se only?] imperfectly.

REV. XII.

In the twelfth chapter of Revelation [is] depicted a remarkable series of his [works.] May the Lord open up to our minds [?]

… existence as a person,
… …ination of his plans, and
… … provided to meet him at

… … into the interpretation of
… however blessed it may be to
… …, and understands it; but I
… to glean a few practical lessons
… truths revealed to us in this pic-
… its details, has yet to be ful-
… …ducing these, I would merely
… characters that figure in the scene,
… these lessons we may not con-
… of the intelligent reader who is
… deeper and closer rendering of it.
… 19, the temple of God is open in
… and His elders are now seen as
… iv.), and *the ark* of His covenant
… of His grace, and the *lightning*
… judgment, before we are intro-
… great scene of chap. xii. We are
… dragon is, verse 9, 'That old ser-
… 'devil and Satan, who deceiveth
… '—like the *aliases* of a habit-and-
… . The man-child, from Ps. ii., Isa.
… Lord Jesus, ver. 5, 'a man-child
… rule all nations with a rod of iron.'
… symbolic language of course, being
… according to the flesh, Christ was
… the faithful remnant persecuted and
… …ough the tribulation of the short
… Satan has been cast out of heaven

(where the saints have been [...]
[...]) to the earth, where he is in [...]
his time is short ere he be chained [...]

I. THE DEVOURER.

Read the 4th verse of this twelfth [...] 'And the Dragon stood before the w[oman] was ready to be delivered, for to de[vour...] as soon as it was born.'

Jesus is said to be 'born king of the [...] Matt. i. Look at chap. ii.: there we [find] devil's first attempt to devour Him as soo[n as he] was born. Herod, his tool, slew 'all the [children] that were in Bethlehem and in all the coast[s there]of from two years old and under,' and the [weep]ing of Rachel is the sad witness to the [devil's] awful power, but through the almighty [hand of] God the young child's life is spared. [Failing] in this murderous plan, he comes with [his] temptation, trying to make Him leave th[e path] of the Sent One and the Servant; but the [word] of God made him flee for a season. W[e see the] great dragon, the serpent, in his last [and] desperate attack on the man-child at [the cross,] bruising His heel, trying to hold Him in [death's] hold, wounding Him with his venom[...]. The devourer feels now sure of his prey[...] is in the jaws of death. Chains of [...] around him. 'Shall the prey be taken [from the] mighty, shall the lawful captive be de[livered?] [Y]es: there is a greater power than the [...], there is the Almighty. There is [...]

...... in Creation or Providence ...... power of coming out from ...... down the life and taking it ...... death He destroyed him ...... of death, that is the devil.' ...... failed to devour the Prince of ...... got his head bruised. This is ...... serpent on the pole, whose power ...... destroyed by the Son of Man lifted ...... The sting has been wrenched ...... jaws. The keys of death and ...... now hung at the girdle of the ...... who has fought the fight ...... weakness showing Himself to be

...... weakness and defeat
...... won the meed and crown;
...... all our foes beneath His feet,
...... being trodden down.

...... hell in hell laid low;
...... Made sin, He sin o'erthrew;
...... Bow'd to the grave, destroy'd it so,
And death by dying slew.'

...... purpose the Son of God was manifested, ... might destroy the works of the devil.' ...... 8.) The Lord is risen, yea, He is ...... a man, a glorified man, beyond the ...... Satan. He is seated as the subject One. ...... who undertook for man has been ...... unto God and to His throne,' and we ...... is the deliverance that is mentioned ...... 5. It is a question now to be settled

between Satan and the God who has r...
Christ between the power of Satan and th...
power of the Almighty God. Justice and...
have vindicated Christ's title to bruise t...
pent's head, and take His position as t...
highest in heaven on God's own throne.

The serpent in Eden tempted the wom...
ruined mankind. God said, 'I will put ...
between thee and the woman, between th...
and her seed.' Blessed be God, He has ...
enmity; and it cannot be taken away. ...
fearful friendship it would have been if G...
left man in the friendship that Adam beg...
Satan! All along the stream of time ...
been at his devouring work. To-day he is ...
about as a roaring lion seeking whom h...
devour.' Do we realize this? It surely ...
something. I believe it means far more t...
suppose. By how many different ways d...
accomplish this? If he can keep people in...
natural state of death, he is as sure of his ...
if he had them with him in everlasting b...
If he can lull them, soothe them, deceive...
blind them, he has them sure, and they wi...
easy prey.

He knows that life is communicat...
Spirit applying the *word of the living* ...
word that tells of a vi...
Christ, of Him who ...
live again for everm...
...ever to Him wh...
...ne, and tells him...

The Devil.

[the] conqueror of death, that he is
[also] death's master. Wherefore Satan is
[busy when] the Gospel of God is preached, so
[that] there is a class of people that hear
[it, and] 'then cometh the devil, and taketh
[the word] out of their hearts, *lest* they should
[believe and] be saved.' (Luke viii. 12.) What a
[devilish] intention! Does every preacher of the
[Gospel realise] this, that such an enemy is among
[his hearers]? Does every hearer realise it, that
[the] seemingly simple thing may leave him in
[the hands of] Satan for ever? If men do not believe
[they] must be born again in order to enter the
[Kingdom] of God, Satan does. If men do not be-
[lieve that] the 'entrance of the word gives light,'
[he does]. He takes this word away *lest* it
[should save] them. Satan is a clever theologian.
[He knows] the Bible, he believes it, he can quote
[it and] use it for his own fiendish ends. After
[the word] is preached, he is ever ready to snatch
[away the] word. 'What did you think of that
[sermon?]' is the common introduction after the
[word is] preached, to a series of criticisms on his
[merits and] demerits, and a pretty sure token that
[in the] discussion concerning the messenger the
[message] is to be forgotten. '*Lest* they should
[believe and] be saved!' If Satan can keep out
[belief,] he will let the man cultivate the field,
[be] attentive to it, water it, spend much time
[in] plain words he will let men be moral
[philanthropic], be religious and make profes-
[sion and contend] stoutly for sound orthodoxy and

clever theology, if he can keep out the seed of life.

Satan knows that there is life in a *look* at the crucified One, therefore he will let the wounded sinner apply ointment and plasters and all sorts of palliatives to his sin-bitten soul; but will use all his power to keep him from beholding the Lamb of God. A look at the brazen serpent cured those bitten by fiery serpents; a look at Him who destroyed the great serpent's power immediately and for ever saves those who are ready to be devoured by the mighty dragon, for 'as Moses lifted up the serpent in the wilderness, even so must the Son of man be lifted up, that whosoever believeth in Him should not perish, but have eternal life.' By many devices the great deceiver succeeds in hiding this life-giving truth, for 'if our gospel be hid it is hid to them that are lost, in whom the *God of this world* hath blinded the minds of them which believe not, lest the light of the glorious gospel of Christ who is the image of God should shine unto them.' Thus, O Appolyon, Abbadon, thou art the deceiver of the whole world. What fools men are! Reader, are you led captive at his will? are you in his meshes, within the teeth of his jaws, ready to be devoured? Are you not only led captive of your lusts, but bound hand and foot by Satan?

Believing reader, in Christ thou art safe, is at God's throne; thou art there in Him; is thy safety. God's throne is safe, he cannot devour it, therefore he cannot devour thee.

... as to devouring thee, he is
... His power is broken. The
... of the great dragon that old ser-
... met and overcome by the 'Lamb
... of the throne.'
... evil one,' 'the wicked one,' thy
... 'The Holy One' is thy preserver.
... angel of the bottomless pit' at thy back
... belching flame? 'The King of Glory'
... of thy salvation.
... knife of him that is 'a murderer from
... ' whetted to be plunged into thy
... 'The Prince of Life' is thy life.
... prince of darkness' trying to enwrap
... 'The Light of Life' surrounds thy

... Satan come as an angel of light? We
... the blessed Spirit, by whom we can
... wiles; we are not ignorant of his
... Let us be sober and vigilant against
... We have to pick our steps. Being
... Christ, soon we shall be 'caught up' in
... body and soul, entirely and for ever
... his power, wiles, devices, and snares.
... shall be caught up together with all the
... God, to meet our Conqueror in the air,
... ever with Him; and 'the God of peace
... bruise Satan under your feet shortly.'
... 20.)
... he is thus foiled, and cannot *devour* us,
... leave us? Nay! But we find Satan in
... twelfth chapter (ver. 10), as

II. THE ACCUSER.

'He ACCUSES the brethren before God day and night.' Michael and his angels are to cast him down to the earth at the beginning of the time of great trial; but meantime he is there, not certainly in 'the light,' God's dwelling-place, in the third, the highest, heaven, but as the Prince of the Power of the Air, having power to stand before God and accuse the brethren. That Satan has access into God's presence may startle some who have not thought about it; but it is the teaching of Scripture. 1 Kings xxii. 21, shews that a lying spirit appeared before God, to put lies into the mouth of Ahab's advisers.

Again in Job i. 6, we read—'Now there was a day when the sons of God came to present themselves before the Lord, and Satan came also among them,' to accuse Job. In Zech. iii. it is written—'He shewed me Joshua the high priest standing before the angel of the Lord and Satan standing at his right hand to resist him.' And Eph. vi. 12—'We wrestle not against flesh and blood, but against . . . spiritual wickedness in *heavenly* places.' Day and night, dear fellow Christians, he has access to God, and accuses before Him; sometimes truly, alas! How often does he first tempt and then accuse! How in a failure of ours can he put his hand upon it; besides he is a slanderer, a false accuser. He is not the accuser of the world, but only of the brethren,' but he 'deceiveth the whole world.'

The Devil.

... our strength? 'If any man sin, we ... advocate with the Father,' One who ... slumbers nor sleeps. We speak much, and ... dwell too much, upon the finished work ... ; but how precious is the finished, untir... unremittent work of our blessed Lord! If ... accuser speaks of sin, He points to the blood, ... which, for us, He has entered into the ...

... 'Jesus Christ the righteous, and He is ... propitiation for our sins.' It is with Him the ... must find fault, for we are in Him. ... short of this appeal to the presented blood ... silence his insinuations and overcome his ... So it is said (ver. 11), 'They over-... him by the *blood* of the Lamb.' Saints do ... him out of heaven—angels do that; but ... brethren overcome him while he is there, and ... them. This is before God.

... own experience of all his accusations I ... the sword of the Spirit, the Word of God, ... from all my feelings and states, and say to ... accusings, as to his temptations, 'It is ...' Thus the Lord Jesus overcame him ... was on earth, therefore it is said that ... 'they overcame him by the blood of the ... but also by 'the *word* of their testimony.' ... the Devil and he will flee from you'—for ... coward at heart; 'neither give place to ...' This latter is spoken with regard to ... From Mark iii. 5, we know that anger is ... but when it passes its just bounds it becomes sinful wrath, and Satan has us in his power. We should not sleep upon our anger. (Eph. iv. 26.)

The blood and the word shut the accuser's mouth for ever, and are the answer to his gravest accusations, be they true or false. Though our sins be as scarlet, Christ points to the blood, and they become 'white as snow;' 'red like crimson,' He says they become as wool. 'If we confess our sins, He is faithful'—why? because His word has said it—'and just'—why? because of the blood presented—'to forgive us our sins, and to cleanse us from all unrighteousness.' The blood of Jesus Christ *cleanseth* us from ALL sin.

Is the father of lies against us?—the living Truth is for us. Is he desiring to sift us as wheat?—The Lord Jesus is constantly praying that our faith may never fail us, for by that shield we can quench all Satan's fiery darts, meet all his accusations, and, in the calm consciousness of eternal peace with God, wait upon Him, do His commandments, and receive the power that shall make us love not our lives unto death. (Rev. xii. 11.)

He cannot *devour* us: we are in Christ.

He is overcome when He *accuses* us; Christ's blood is for us. But does he leave us? No. He exercises his power against us now, as

III. THE PERSECUTOR.

Read Rev. xii. 13. 'When the dragon saw he was cast unto the earth he *persecuted*

And here his cunning is taxed to its
… varying with times and peoples, tastes
… …ation. His manner changes, but the
… … of his sting is always the same—the
… from his mouth always poured upon us.
… into his service all kinds of tools; the
… the inquisition, the scaffold in one age;
… but as real persecution in another;
… will and planning of the world, and what
… than all, the evil-speaking and slandering
… Christians. Individually, beloved friends,
… … are we washing one another's feet, or
… Satan's work, being used as his tools in
… evil of those things that we know not?
… know what it is to be misunderstood, mis-
… …ted, maligned, looked at with suspicion
… …low-Christian, and may have felt it to be
… … persecution, more painful than thumb-
… —watch and pray lest you in turn be thus
… …inst others. We do not feel the reality
… common adversary, else we should be all
… united and of one accord continuing in
… …ly love. Soldiers may have their disputes,
… and even duels, when in barracks and on
… …rvice, but on the battle-field the bitterest
… …lder to shoulder against one common foe.

… all his persecutions, what is the pro-
… ver. 14: power for flight to the wilderness,
… fed there by God. He has given us of
… the spirit of truth and sonship, He has
… into the wilderness, and there we have

found Himself our provision. A quaint old divine used to say, 'the devil acts like a bull-dog to bark at us and drive us closer to Christ'. The Psalms are the experience of David in the place of the poor man in the wilderness finding his all in God. What a blessed thing that Satan's persecutions but drive us nearer to our only good! The wilderness is the happiest place, when we get there from the hand of our living, loving Father, His own manna, His own drink, and the guidance of His pillar cloud. Christ is all.

> 'In the desert, God will teach thee,
>   What the God that thou hast found;
> Patient, gracious, powerful, holy,
>   All His grace shall there abound.
>
> 'Though thy way be long and dreary,
>   Eagle strength He'll still renew;
> Garments fresh, and feet unweary,
>   Tell how God hath brought thee through.'

To be alone with God—to be in the wilderness with God—to be fed by God; is this not life, is this not joy? It was better to be with David on the lonely hill-side, than with Saul in his courtly palaces. Manna, water, and guidance are all I need; what more could I take, for this is Christ, God's own joy, God's own delight, God's own new day by day, new every day; it cannot be kept till to-morrow, yesterday's will not do for to-day. How the hatred of the devil brings glory to God!

His *devourings* bring us to the 'caught up' Christ, the Christ 'received up into glory,' and is thus met by *life in victory*.

His *accusations* bring us to the 'blood of the Lamb,' and are met by *life taken for us.*

His *persecutions* bring us to the wilderness provisions, and are met by *life nourished.*

After all this we have nothing more to fear, we can fear no evil, God is with us, as above and independent of all circumstances we find God for us, a table spread in the wilderness in presence of our enemies. He may still show his venom after he is thoroughly defeated, for we next find him as

IV. THE BLASPHEMER.

This is seen in Rev. xiii. 5, 6, in the person of the beast to whom Satan gives power. 'He opened his mouth in blasphemy against God to blaspheme His name, and His tabernacle, and them that dwell in heaven.' But blasphemies can do us little harm. We need no fortification against them. At school we have seen the big boy that used to lord it over all the little ones, subdued, conquered, and on the ground. In his defeat he could only call bad names which he knew could do no harm. Even though Satan slay the body, he touches not our life—it is hid with Christ in God. Can he devour that? It is because of the name we bear that the blasphemies of hell are poured upon us. There are the 'synagogues of Satan,' in which the blasphemous doctrines of devils are taught. We fear not the servants of Satan, though homage on all sides be paid to him by all classes, in their business and pleasure, and the crowns of earth be laid at his feet.

Those whose names are written from the foundation of the world in the book of the Lamb slain, can listen to his blasphemies, and can rejoice in the Lord, though he should slay their bodies; they can afford to wait for their inheritance.

What can I now say, unsaved sinner to you? You are in the *jaws of the devil*. He is your father; is he to be your tormentor day and night for ever in that awful hell which was never prepared for you, but 'for the devil and his angels'? Look at the judgment of the living nations, the contrast between the blessing and cursing—'blessed of my Father,' but not 'cursed of my Father'—'Kingdom prepared for you,' but 'fire prepared for the devil and his angels.' One look outward to Christ and you are saved; not a look inward to a feeling that can give nothing but despair to the conscientious soul. God has given you the Lord Jesus Christ and in Him is all. Are you not satisfied with Christ? God is.

Fellow believer, rejoice in the Lord. The power of our greatest enemy is broken: soon will be really, and as to fact, as he is already judicially and to faith, bruised beneath thy feet. Christ is thine, and all His power, and dominion, and might, and glory, and inheritance, are thine; and, above all, His heart, His love, Himself, thine.

In Him we conquer the devourer;
In Him we overcome the accuser;
In Him we defy the persecutor;
In Him we are beyond the blasphemer. 'More than conquerors through Him that loved us.'

Come with your weakness and find shelter in the all-powerful Jehovah.

Eph. vi. 11-18.

Be strong in Jehovah, though hard be the fight,
We'll conquer, we know, in the power of His might;
Put on the whole armour of God every one,
For it alone shelters till victory's won.

Thus we sing while we march through the midst of our foes,
Who stand all determined our way to oppose;
We shall conquer their legion, our battle-song raise;
The Lord is our Captain; His name ever praise.

Thus armed we shall stand and shall meet Satan's wiles.
We know his devices, the world he beguiles;
It is not against flesh and blood that we fight,
But powers that would force us from heavenly light.

With loins girt with truth may we stand in the fight,
And righteousness placed as our breastplate so bright;
Our feet shod with sandals prepared for the war,
The gospel of peace which our foes shall not mar.

Above all Faith's shield we must grasp 'gainst our foes,
By it we shall quench every dart Satan throws;
Salvation our helmet, bestowed by our Lord,
The sword of the Spirit His conquering word.

The trumpet is sounding, the trumpet of war,
Not peace while we wait for our bright morning Star,
We watch where the foe would surprise or alarm,
By prayer we shall nerve for the fight every arm.

Lord, give us more faith thus to meet every foe,
Thus Satan is conquered and shall be laid low,
This, this, is the triumph o'er earth and its gain,
O'er sin still within but which never shall reign.

'Serving the Lord.'

OUR WORK.

I WAS very much interested, in reading the life of Dr Thomas Chalmers, to see how many years he preached the gospel to others, and yet, by his own confession, was still unconverted. One of the most solemn texts to be found in Scripture is, Matt. vii. 22, 'Many will say to me in that day Lord, Lord, have we not prophesied in Thy name? and in Thy name have cast out devils, and in Thy name done many wonderful works. And then, will I profess unto them, I never knew you: depart from me ye that work iniquity.'

A man may preach with the most powerful eloquence, and may be used to do God's work, and may still be unsaved. The Lord tells us there will be 'many' such. He does not say that He once knew them, and that they went back: He says, 'I *never* knew you.' Reader, are you among the number. Many in this Christian land begin very early to engage in some good work. At a certain time, they become members of the church, as it is called: how often, alas! not knowing whether they are saved or not. They then take, perhaps, a class in the Sabbath-school, have a district to visit, look after the affairs of the church, or the necessities of the poor, attain

... the position of a deacon or an elder,
... of a preacher, and all this time they may
have had this matter definitely, finally,
... settled, 'Am I saved?' They trust
... on the right road to be saved, which, of
... is the leading idea in all legalism, ritualism,
popery, and an entire ignoring of the Bible
...

... do the best they can, and strive it may
... prayers and tears and resolutions and
... *in order* to get into God's favour,
... by in the long run to receive eternal
... the pardon of all their sins.
... work and do the best they can, and
... the former do, but it is *because* they
... *are* accepted already—*because* they
... *have* the pardon of all their sins—
... they know that they *have* eternal life.
... is false service, the latter is true.

I. FALSE SERVICE.

... are those who believe in justification by
... other doctrines of grace, and who yet
... if they do their duty, and try to serve
... sincerely and faithfully as they can, He
... last overlook their many failures in some
way or other for Christ's sake, and reward
... the good deeds which they have done,
... them at the judgment day everlasting life.
... this is quite a mistake, and arises from a
misapprehension of God's character and
condition. God's character is perfect, and

before I can be engaged in acceptable service I must be in harmony with this character. In order to be a proper servant of God, I must *start with being perfectly accepted* by God.

Man's position is not that of one who is only a little out of God's mind, and who by a few sincere and vigorous efforts may be put right; but of one who is really dead, so far as connection with God is concerned. He is separated from God, and therefore from truth, from goodness, from life. In God is all truth, all goodness, all life; outside of Him there is none. Man by nature is born out of fellowship with God, and therefore he has not the slightest power to serve God acceptably, for he has not the life that can move in the direction of God, and in which he can serve Him. The movements in Christian service of an unconverted man are the galvanic movements of a corpse which may seem very energetic, yet, alas! it is but a corpse that moves! All Scripture and experience tell us these two truths concerning God's character and man's condition.

Wherefore, dear friend, unless thou hast been born again, quickened into a new life from death, thou canst not serve God acceptably. Thou mayest strive day and night in all sincerity, but thou art dead; thou mayest visit the sick and minister to the dying (the holiest privileges of a saved one); all is vain; thou mayest comfort and assist the widow and the fatherless, and have the prayers of many an orphan for thy reward, and yet be no better as to thy standing before God

… and the profane; thou mayest … to the poor; thou mayest support … Christ in all its missions and churches … abroad; thou mayest give half of thy … the advancement of the Lord's work, … penny stand to thy credit before God. … sacrifice, beautiful, fair, and lovely as it was, … by a man who was at that time a … of religion, and a sincere worshipper, was … by God. And so it is still. God will … and your sacrifice unless you come as … with Him through *His* sacrifice, and … coming to make friends with God by … sacrifice. If you are out of Christ, your … as well as your *bad* deeds are an … to God. All your '*righteousnesses* are … rags' (Isa. lxiv. 6), not only failing to … but *defiling* you. '*Whatsoever* is not … sin.' (Rom. xiv. 23.) You may be true to … ; you may do your duty as parents, … for your own; but it is all sin: for, as … Scripture, 'the ploughing of the wicked … (Prov. xxi. 4.) Every action, however … in the Christian, and however binding … as a moral duty, is reckoned by God, … an unbeliever, to be a sin, because it is … of one not at peace with Him through … peace. 'Without faith it is impossible to …' (Heb. xi. 6.) This is God's theology, … hard it may seem, and however much … your ideas and to the prevailing ideas … concerning good works and their reward. *'Dead works'* is stamped on all your deeds. Until you can serve God as one who is saved, all your service will but intensify your anguish in the pit of woe, whither the Christless, the seemingly good and fair, beautiful and noble, are all swept together with the vile, the loathsome, the idolator, and the profane. There are not two hells. Where will you spend eternity?

II. TRUE SERVICE.

Half an hour ago you may have been serving in the dark, as an unforgiven one, and during the next half hour you may pass from death unto life, and thus stand on the ground of the accepted servant. God is perfect: to meet God I must meet Him in perfection. There is no perfection in me; but He has provided the means by which each of us may at once become acceptable servants, by first becoming accepted *sons*. His only-begotten and well-beloved Son, eternally in the Father's bosom, took upon Him our nature, descended to our place of responsibility and service, and approved Himself to be the perfect Servant, in that very place in which we had failed; made sin for us, was obedient unto death, having gone through all the billows of God's wrath, raised from the dead, and is now at the Father's right hand. If, therefore, we become by faith identified with Him, we can see in Him all our responsibilities under law met; we can look into His empty grave, and reckon our sins buried,

'Serving the Lord.'

... now, as those who are beyond the ... and beyond its judgment, we can ... 'newness of life,' a life in resurrection. ... nothing else, is the foundation of true ... the service of love, the service of sons; ... now stand in Christ's place of sonship as ... in grace occupied our place of death.

... ask you, is this not a real vantage ground ... ? What a wretched, menial service it ... be working hard for life, and doubting ... it can ever be obtained! The true ser... working *from* the Cross not *to* the Cross. ... does not bestir itself to get life, but ... man first works because he has life ... received. This is God's plan; *life*, then ...

Ask yourself now the question, 'Am I ... because I have life, because I am saved?' ... is evident that you *know* you are saved— ... that you are of God.' (1 John v. 19.) ... perhaps some one may be thinking, 'Well, ... doing this little and that little, but I ... never been conscious of being born again.' ... dear friend at once, and make it sure. ... instantly from thy service, and get rid of ... by believing in Him who, as the perfect ... 'bare our sins in His own body on the ... (1 Peter ii. 24.) Get into Christ—in His ... thou canst meet and serve the living

... you may ask, 'How am I to get into ... simply by knowing Him (John xvii. 3); ... on Him (John iii. 36;) by trusting

Q

in Him (2 Tim. i. 12.) You do not require to go to heaven to beseech God to send you Christ to die for sin. (Rom. x. 6.) No! 'For God so loved the world that He *gave* His only-begotten Son.' (John iii. 16.) And Christ dieth no more. In the love-gift of God, Christ is yours. If you go to hell, it must be over *a given Christ*.

When the poor men in the cotton manufacturing districts were starving, money was gathered, and sent to the committee for distributing bread to them. Now, suppose some poor man, with his wife and children sitting in their empty room, the last of their furniture having been sold for bread; a few stones for seats, and a bunch of straw for their bed; no fire on the hearth; not a crust of bread in the cupboard, children crying for bread; the mother's eyes refusing to weep; the father's skeleton hands clasped in anguish; no food, and no work; starvation they have staring them in the face! A knock is heard at the door, a man comes in with a loaf and lays it on the table, and says, '*That is yours, for the* people of Britain have so pitied you that they have sent this bread. Rise, eat, rejoice, and starve no more.' Suppose that poor man would neither touch the loaf himself, nor let his wife nor children taste it, saying, 'How can it be mine? I never got a pennyworth of bread but by the sweat of my brow; there must be some mistake, I cannot take this; not having wrought for it, it cannot be mine.' Everybody would say, '*Eat, man! eat*, and ask no questions, for you are

'Serving the Lord.'

[...] and the messenger's word is enough. [...] the loaf is yours.'

[...]-sinner, this is but a faint picture of *your* [...] and *God's provision*. CHRIST, His [...] provision for the soul's need, *has been* sent, [...] for sin, and has gone back in right- [...] to the Father. Are you not on the edge [...] damnation, and do you begin to ask [...] about your warrant to take Christ? [...] is only for a sinner. Yea more, God [...] you to use Him. (1 John iii. 23.) [...] disobey God by continuing unsaved?

How can I serve the Lord until I can say, 'He [...] Lord?'

[...] gentleman had paid his money for the ran- [...] of a slave, and had given her her freedom. [...] had been born a slave, and knew not what [...] meant. Her tears fell fast on the signed [...] which her deliverer brought to prove [...]; she only looked at him with fear. At [...] got ready to go his way, and as he told [...] she must do when he was gone, it did [...] on her what freedom was. With the first [...] 'I will follow him,' she said, 'I will follow [...] will serve him all my days;' and to every [...] against it she only cried, 'He redeemed [...] redeemed me! He redeemed me!'

[...] strangers used to visit that master's [...] noticed, as all did, the loving constant [...] of the glad-hearted girl, and asked her [...] was so eager with unbidden service.

night by night, and day by day, she had but one answer, and she loved to give it—

'HE REDEEMED ME! HE REDEEMED ME! HE REDEEMED ME!'

Is this *your* motive-power for serving God— 'He redeemed me?'—or is it only, 'Well, I hope I may yet be found among the redeemed, and meanwhile I do the best I can?' Wretched slavery, with the chain of death or doubt hanging on the limbs! Rather take God at His word now, and joyfully exclaim, 'O Lord, truly I am Thy servant. . . . Thou hast loosed my bonds' (Psalm cxvi. 16.)

III. A WORD TO FELLOW-SERVANTS.

I would now speak a word to you who are fellow-workers for, and fellow-sufferers with, Christ. It is only now that we can have fellowship with Him in His service as the rejected of earth. Let us then be 'instant in season, out of season.'

'*He redeemed me!*' Let it be written as with letters of gold on every page of our diary. While in your mission of love you visit the poor, the sick, and the dying, may it ever be your first work to point them to Christ. While in every way striving to alleviate misery, even if it were by giving but a cup of cold water, let the main thing be to speak of Christ. Be careful ever to have the single eye, and do nothing to be seen of men. Do nothing to men; do all to God; and have no master but your Redeemer. Be bold

... by no chain but that of love. If a great ... be denied you, occupy the small one. If ... yours to preach to hundreds or thousands, ... Him who spent a sultry noon under a ... sun by the well side, that He might impart the water of life to a worthless woman. 'Whatsoever thy hand findeth to do, do it with thy might;' do not wait for to-morrow and for the great opportunity, but do the little service, whatever it may be, do it *now*. Draw all your strength from God, depending on Him alone.

The great work is that which is done on individual responsibility—'My own work.' Our Lord says 'Whatsoever ye shall ask the Father in my name He will give you.' (John xvi. 23.) '*Whatsoever*,' without limit, without restraint, without bound, so that we may ask anything you please. Fellow-worker with God, do you feel as if this were too much, and say 'I cannot have God's arm so under my will?' It is nevertheless true. What! can a creature thus prevail with the Creator? Yes indeed, and the reason is, that we have been made 'partakers of the divine nature' (2 Pet. i. 4), because before God we are as Christ is—as near, as dear. We are in Him, and being in Him, every request, proceeding from the Holy Ghost in us, is in perfect harmony with the Divine Mind.

We may well say with such a petition, What grace, Lord! what condescension! what love! Thou hast not spared Thy Son! Thou hast made me one with Him. Thou hast said, whatsoever I will I shall receive; and Therefore, Lord, my will is *whatsoever Thou wilt.* I give thee back Thy behest. It is too much for me to bear, and now, from the very depths of my soul, I pray, 'Father Thy will be done! Lead me in Thy will; may everything I do be in Thy mind;' and then, *asking* will but be the promptings of the Holy Spirit within me, and *receiving* but the natural issue from the hand of Him who Himself inspired the prayer. What a service of joy! Such a life has no outward bustle and noise, no running hither and thither, but, like the light, it cannot be hid. Quietly it beams wherever it exists. It is calm as the gentle heat of the summer sun noiselessly warming all around. Thus energised by the life from above, meet parent and child, friend and neighbour, rich and poor, and the brighter will be your 'crown of righteousness.' Servants faithful to their earthly masters shall receive the reward of the inheritance at the judgment-seat of Christ. (Col. iii. 24.) It will then appear that it was better to have spoken 'five words' (1 Cor. xiv. 19) to God, than to have spoken 'ten thousand words' to make 'a fair shew in the flesh' (Gal. vi. 12), and please men; better to have been eloquent to God in the calm silence of a life pointing to Christ, than to have made earth ring with high-sounding words and world-patching schemes.

'It was not any word that was ever spoken to me,' said an old and oft-approved servant of God to a brother in the Lord from whom I heard the narrative; 'it was not any word that wakened me up from my death of sin, but the movement of

...finger. My mother had often prayed
... tried to lead me to Christ; but I
... and when I escaped from her control
... wild sinner and such a bold infidel
... godly friends were afraid to see me;
... providence of God, I was left to watch
... the bedside of a tailor, a poor deformed
... when he lay a-dying. He had often
... me of Christ, but I had never heeded
... more than my mother, or any of the
... When I was nursing him there that day,
... with me many times to mind my soul,
... perfectly hard; all he could say had no
... But at last when the death-rattle was in
... and I saw he could speak no longer, he
... his hand and pointed with his finger
... *That* stirred me, and I had no rest
... gave me rest.'
... judgment-seat is coming. Fellow Chris-
... question will be raised there about thy
... about thy salvation. As to safety thou
... passed from death unto life, and wilt
... into judgment; but as to service, thy
... be judged. The judgment is by fire.
... stands that trial stands to thy credit—
... stands, then thy works will all be lost
... thyself art saved as by fire.
... two kinds of works—one class sym-
... scripture under the heading of wood,
... ; the other, gold, silver, precious
... every work is on the one side or the
... will observe that wood, hay, and

stubble are greater in quantity. But it is not quantity that the fire regards; a ton of hay is as easily and as surely burned as a pound. Many in our day have the greatest regard for quantity—great works, much activity. How little the striving after the pure gold, the silver, and the precious stones! How mixed is the life-work of the best man! A layer of wood, a grain of gold, then a large quantity of hay, then a little silver, plenty of stubble, how few precious stones: but the fire sifts all! At that awful catastrophe at Abergele, where railway carriages and living men and women were burned to ashes, diamonds, gold watches and silver ornaments were found afterwards among the rubbish. The peer could not be distinguished from the servant; wood could not be separated from bone; but the diamond was still bright, and the gold and silver still precious. What a happy day is coming for every Christian! He will be so glad to see in one blaze, as upon one funeral pile, all that in his life ever dishonoured his Lord, or was not done with the single eye: only that will reappear in glory, which was to God's glory here, and he, already glorified, can at that tribunal appreciate nothing but what is in harmony with glory.

When at school our great ambition was to be first in the class. Who will be first then of all the class of Christians? Very different will be God's order then from our order now! The great of earth and preachers (even those who were of greatest eminence) perhaps giving place to some

... starving widow, or some little child. I ... that many of those who are called ... known and honoured Christians, will ... day, as to reward for the single eye, be ... some poor weak, despised ones of earth, ... power was in the secret place with God. ... with righteous judgment.

... Christian, what of thy gold then? will it ... stubble in the glory? or art thou ... it now into the currency of heaven? ... to travel in a foreign land, I could not ... very well with my British money. Even ... those coming from Scotland find it ... to exchange Scotch notes. Before we go ... we change as much money as we may re... into the coin of that realm. Friend, this is ... thy life here is still given: 'make to ... friends of the mammon of unrighteous... that when ye fail they may receive you into ... habitations.' So said the Master, and ... disciples have wondered and not understood ... passage. It is simply 'exchange your money ... currency of heaven.'

... mammon of unrighteousness;' that is to ... the Jewish economy it was a sign of a ... man that his basket and store were full, ... had plenty of cattle, that he was rich. ... since Christ's rejection it is not so. The ... have God's money in this age. The ... lot of the Christian is poverty; nowhere ... the head, since there was 'no room in the ... for the Master. But suppose a man with a large fortune is converted, what is he to do with this mammon of unrighteousness? Is he to hoard it up and add to it, and die a rich man? Nay. Is he at once and heedlessly to throw it away? Nay. He is to make it his friend. Exchange it into the coin of heaven. If he waits till he dies, none can be put into his coffin to arise with him. But there is a method of sending it on before: the Lord has taught it. How many cups of cold water can it buy? These count, if given with the single eye. How many Bibles and missionaries to the heathen? Ten thousand channels are easily found when wanted. Whatever you do, make your money not your enemy, as it will be if you use it for self, but your friend, so that when you are done with money it may not be done with you, but will be standing to meet you in a new dress, in the gold and silver and precious stones at the throne, in the 'well done' of the Master. Poor brother, thy poverty is no bar. One talent well used is more than ten abused, and money is but a poor talent.

It is not an occasional or periodic earnestness that God desires, but a calm, constant life-long work. A man moving about this world with the Holy Ghost within him, prepared for anything at every step, by every look and word, testifying for his Lord, conscious of no effort, but living in calm peace with his Saviour God, in the unhindered power of an inner life, in the patient hope of a glory soon to dawn, is the type of God's true servant. His service does not depend on

... his circumstances, his position: these are
... subservient to what the man is. He may be
... wealthiest in the world, or have to sweep a
... but his joy in the service is the same.
... will have a natural entrance into the courts
... where the servants serve their Lord day
... night.

'O send me forth, my Saviour,
  O send me for Thy glory,
Regarding not the praise of man,
And trampling on the fear of man,
  And fighting for Thy glory, Thy glory.

There is a man who often stands
  Between me and Thy glory,
    His name is self,
    My carnal self,
    Self-seeking self,
Stands 'twixt me and Thy glory.

O mortify him, mortify him,
  Put him down, my Saviour,
Exalt Thyself alone: lift high
  The banner of the cross,
    And in its folds
Conceal the standard-bearer.'

... Lord has many servants in different spheres.
... given pastors, teachers, and evangelists,
... giving each member in the body his own
... work. The following, in the words of
... gives us a high ideal of the New Testa-
... evangelist:—'The missionary after the
... school is a man without a purse, with-
... without a change of raiment, without
... without the care of making friends or

keeping friends, without the hope or desire of worldly good, without the apprehension of worldly loss, without the care of life, without the fear of death; of no rank, of no country, of no condition; a man of one thought—the gospel of Christ; a man of one purpose—the glory of God; a fool, and content to be reckoned a fool, for Christ; a madman, and content to be reckoned a madman, for Christ.

'Let him be enthusiast, fanatic, babbler, or any other outlandish nondescript the world may choose to denominate him. But still let him be a nondescript, a man that cannot be classed under any of their categories, or defined by any of their convenient or conventional names. When they can call him pensioner, trader, householder, citizen; man of substance, man of the world, man of science, man of learning, or even man of common sense, it is all over with his missionary character. He may innocently have some of these forms of character, some of them he cannot innocently have; but they will be far, subordinate, deep in the shade, covered, and extinguished to the world's incurious gaze, by the strange, inodinate, and unaccountable character to which he surrendereth himself mainly.

'The world knoweth the missionary not, because it knew Messiah not. The nature of his life is hid with Christ in God; he is not a man, but the spirit of a man; he is a spirit that hath divested itself of all earthiness; save the continent body, which it keepeth down and under

'Serving the Lord.'

tabernacle and its vehicle and its mechanical
... for speech and for action.'

Every child of God, great and small, has a
work; his or her own work. A brother in the
Lord greatly surprised an old bed-ridden follower
of the Lord by coming in with a smile to her one
day and saying,

'I've got some work for you to do.'

'Me! what work! what can I do?'

'Oh, there's a little district meeting to be
started, and you are to have special charge of it in
praying about it.'

She got deeply interested in the people attending
the little meeting, and this work did her and
them much good. I saw a young boy confined
to bed one day, and I told him he had a work to
do. He had found Christ, but he looked a little
surprised. 'You have to pray and preach,' I said.
He smiled in surprise.—'Yes, you have to pray
for those that carry forth the gospel, and you
have to lie there and preach sermons to all that
come in, sermons on faith, patience, meekness,
gentleness, adorning on your back, as we on our
feet ought to do, the doctrine of God our Saviour.
The same thought came also from the lips of
another young disciple, now in the presence of the
Lord, waiting the resurrection beauty in which he
will be clothed with all those who have been
faithful unto death—who have endured to the
end. He said, 'We *all* must speak for Jesus,'
when it was suggested that some might be too
young to bear testimony to Christ.

Listen to what God says He has done for you, and then begin to do something for God.

"'Not your own!' but His ye are,
 Who hath paid a price untold
For your life, exceeding far
 All earth's store of gems and gold.
With the precious blood of Christ,
Ransom treasure all unpriced,
Full redemption is procured,
Full salvation is assured.

'Not your own!' but His by right,
 His peculiar treasure now,
Fair and precious in His sight,
 Purchased jewels for His brow.
He will keep what thus He sought,
Safely guard the dearly bought,
Cherish that which He did choose,
Always love and never lose.

'Not your own!' To Him ye owe
 All your life and all your love;
Live, that ye His praise may show,
 Who is yet all praise above.
Every day and every hour,
Every gift and every power,
Consecrate to Him alone,
Who hath claimed you for His own.

Teach us, Master, how to give
 All we have and are to Thee;
Grant us, Saviour, while we live,
 Wholly, only, Thine to be.
Henceforth be our calling high
Thee to serve and glorify:
Ours no longer, but Thine own,
Thine for ever, Thine alone!"

Judgment.

OUR REWARD,

'I DO not think that we can know we are saved till the judgment day.'

'But it matters very little what we think, for God says that His Bible is written that we may *know* that we have eternal life.' (1 John v. 13.) This is the answer to such a false and absurd statement; God's word was written that we might antedate the judgment day and know its issues now. Do you think that the Apostle Paul, after having been 1800 years with the Lord, is to wait at the judgment day to know whether he is saved or not? This is most evidently absurd. In John v. 20-30 we get the whole point settled by infinite wisdom. If you have not passed from death unto life down here below, and are not thus standing in the rank of those who 'shall not come into judgment,' you will be damned to all eternity. As the tree falls it lies. The Godly man cries, 'enter not into judgment with Thy servant, for in Thy sight shall no man living be justified.' (Psalm cxliii. 2.) Through death and resurrection in Christ, as those who have been judged and justified, we are prepared for eternity. From the above mistake, however, some are often inclined to flee to another.

256 *Judgment.*

'How can I be judged after I am saved?' the answer to this question is.

'God says, "*we* must *all* appear before the judgment-seat of Christ that *every one* may receive the things done in his body, according to that he hath done, whether it be good or bad" (2 Cor. 10,) also "Why dost thou judge thy brother? why dost thou set at nought thy brother? *we* shall all stand before the judgment-seat of Christ." (Romans xiv. 10.) These statements are perfectly reconcilable with the precious truth that the believer 'shall not come into judgment.' We shall never be judged as to whether we are saved or lost, but every deed we have done shall be judged, deeds we have forgotten, deeds we did not know we had done. Those who are in Christ will rejoice to see all their rubbish burned. Oh then will they know what grace has done for them; then they shall receive their reward. Those not in Christ shall be destroyed with their works. 'If the righteous scarcely be saved, where shall the ungodly and the sinner appear?' We are justified by faith; we are judged according to our works. Many, even Christians, forget this and think that because, as to justification, judicially our sins are blotted out, therefore there can be no judgment. This is most unscriptural. We are saved as to our persons, but we must all appear before the judgment-seat of Christ, and every motive shall then receive its exact value. 'What manner of persons ought we to be?' Is it not practical infidelity on this point that

Christians often to be careless? Beware! God is not mocked: whatsoever a man sows that shall he also reap.

I. THE SON OF GOD HEALING.

In the beginning of John v. we see the contrast between the quickening power of Christ and the weakness of legal ordinance, in the history of the infirm man at the pool of Bethesda, who had the desire for health, but not the power to profit by the occasional means—the angel's visit. To will was present with him, but to perform he could not. How like a man under law: 'But what the law could not do, in that it was weak through the flesh,' God did in Christ. The Lord Jesus came to the powerless one, and by His word cured him: 'Arise, take up thy bed and walk.' Strength came on the spot. Here is the life manifested now, God manifest in the flesh—*the Son of God.*

II. THE SON OF MAN REJECTED.

The Jews, thinking themselves far better than Christ, sought to kill Him because He wrought on the Sabbath. He showed that God could not rest amid sin and misery, and that He and the Father were one. The Jews sought to kill Him. What a marvel! God manifest in the flesh could become the victim of man's hatred! The Creator submitted to be killed by the creature! Yes; for He was *the Son of man.*

The Lord now shows them the whole truth concerning the matter. He was not another God, but in full union with the Father; doing 'nothing of Himself' (there cannot be two independent supreme Beings), 'but what He seeth the Father do;' and there is nothing that the Father does which He does not show the Son. Christ speaks of Himself as God. He also speaks of Himself as in a position to do the Father's will as the perfect servant who can be seen of men.

III. CHRIST, THE QUICKENER AND JUDGE.

To show His glory in so doing, He speaks of two things (verses 21, 22) :—' He *quickeneth* whom He will;' and the Father hath 'committed all *judgment* unto the Son.' As Son of God He giveth *life*; but as Son of man He may be 'rejected,' 'disallowed,' 'disowned,' 'despised,' 'dishonoured,' therefore ' the Father judgeth no man, but hath committed *all judgment* unto the Son, that all (even His rejecters) should honour the Son, even as they honour the Father.' If we do not receive Him in grace, we must honour Him by being judged by Him; and all are divided into these two classes. Men have many distinctions in society —high and low, rich and poor, old and young, good, bad, indifferent, very good, very bad; but the great division of mankind before God, is into those who have been *quickened* by Christ, the Son of God, or who shall come into *judgment*, under Christ, the Son of Man. To which class do you belong? There must be no mistake on this point, for a slip here is fatal for ever. God has left no doubt about the means of knowing it.

has given us a perfect test by which we may know infallibly, emphasised by a double '*verily*' from the mouth of incarnate Truth.

IV. EVERY BELIEVER HATH EVERLASTING LIFE.

'Verily, verily, I say unto you he that heareth My word, and believeth Him that sent Me, *hath* everlasting life.' '*He* that heareth my word.' This is the word that brought order out of chaos, light out of darkness. This is the word that made myriads of stars revolve around their centres. This is the word that formed man and beast, and tree and rock, that formed 'the sea' and the 'dry land.' This is the word that Jairus' daughter heard as she lay on her couch in the sleep of death. This is the word that the son of the weeping widow heard at Nain's gate, as he was being carried out on his bier. This is the word that Lazarus heard as he lay rotting in his tomb, and, hearing, which he came forth a living man. Whosoever now hears that word, and trusts that Father who sent Christ, by believing this life-giving word, '*hath* everlasting life.' Anxious soul, you have often said, Would that I could see Him with these eyes, I would draw from Him one word that would give me life! Would that I could see Him walking past my door, I would rush out and grasp His robe and be healed, as the poor woman was who touched His garment. Yes, but is His word not the same now, and far more important to us? that blessed Word which His Spirit of truth has written about Him, and whispers into your soul concerning Him!

For say not in thine heart who shall ascend up into heaven to bring Christ down? He *has come down*, or who shall descend to the grave to bring Him up? He *is* risen, He is gone above. But His *word* is in thy mouth and in thy heart, and will it not satisfy you—His word, which is nigh to you, close to you, 'the word of salvation which we preach?' 'Hear, and your soul shall live.' What a contradiction! Can metaphysics explain it? Can man's reason fathom it? Yet we believe it. Man's line is too short for man's need, but he that believeth '*hath everlasting life.*' It is not a life on probation (as Adam's, which could be lost), but *everlasting* life, Christ's own life; for it is 'no longer I, but *Christ that liveth in me.*' It is not '*shall have,*' but 'HATH.' It is not the promise of a future blessing at the last day, but the gift and present possession of *life now! Heareth, believeth, hath*; what a gospel for poor dead sinners! We need no longer wait at 'pools,' for Christ has come down; no longer do we seek and are unable to find, for He has come 'to seek and to save' the lost. He has come to undertake for those that are 'without strength.' What dishonour then can there be like doubting His 'WORD!' The devil says, *Dare you believe* such good news? The Holy Ghost says, *Dare you doubt it?* The devil says, It would be presumption to hear His word, as if it were for *you*. The Holy Ghost says it is just for *you*, and it would be the highest presumption, and a resisting of Him, to stop your ears.

V.—BEYOND DEATH AND JUDGMENT NOW.

Besides having *life*, he that 'heareth and believeth' has something more. 'He shall not come into *judgment*.' (It is the same word in the Greek as at verse 22, and should be so translated.) Why? Because '*He is passed from death unto life.*' The everlasting life that we in believing get is a life in resurrection, life in a risen Christ. What a wonderful truth from our Lord's own lips! 'Shall not come into judgment,' as touching my guilt, my sins, my standing as a living man descended from the first Adam, but reckoned as condemned, judged, dead, buried, and now '*alive unto* God,' already in Christ on resurrection ground. This in no way interferes with our appearance as Christians before the tribunal of Christ for judgment concerning our actions as believers (2 Cor. v.); where we shall get reward, according to the just judgment of our Lord and Master—a most blessed, solemn, and sanctifying thought; but it places the believer, as to his standing, on new ground, beyond the judgment of sin, beyond its doom, beyond his death, in a new life, in which he can now serve God, in which he can stand with joy at that tribunal. How different is God's religion from man's notions of it! Man thinks that God's religion is at best a mere preparation for death and judgment; whereas our blessed Teacher shews us, in this 'word' of His, that it is a *life beyond death and beyond judgment!* Christian, stand up alive unto God. Start up from thy sleep a living man! Thou shalt not come into judgment, but art passed *from death unto life*. All hearers of His word, who trust in Him, have this immunity, whether they *realise* it or not. The word of the Lord has settled all, and it is blasphemy to doubt it. Have you heard Him speak? You may have heard men preach the gospel. Have you really heard good news for yourself from God Himself?

VI.—THE TWO HOURS.

In the fifth chapter of John, our Lord points to TWO PERIODS in which His power is manifested, and speaks of the two classes of people on whom that power is displayed. 'The *hour* is coming, and now is, when the dead shall hear the voice of the *Son of God*, and they that hear shall live.' Man was dead spiritually by sin, he is dead in sin, and the *Son of God* came and quickened him. The hour was *then*, and is going on still, in which He is causing the dead to hear His voice and live. Thousands have been saved in this hour by hearing the voice of the *Son of God*. For the Father hath given Christ, as the *Son of God* manifested here in the flesh, 'to have life in Himself;' 'for,' said John, 'the life was manifested, and we have seen it, and bear witness, and shew unto you that eternal life which was with the Father, and was manifested unto us.' But do not wish to receive Him, all will not hear Him; the most part reject, disown, cast Him out. To meet this state of things, the Father 'hath given Him authority to execute judgment also because He is the *Son of man*.'

As 'Son of man,' He was despised and dishonoured; as 'Son of man,' He shall claim His kingdom; as 'Son of man,' He shall 'execute judgment upon His rejectors;' as 'Son of man,' all nations shall be gathered before Him for judgment; as 'Son of man,' He shall break His foes with a rod of iron; as 'Son of man,' He shall 'reign in righteousness;' as 'Son of man,' He shall sit on the 'great white throne,' and before Him shall stand 'the dead, small and great.' Grace, love, mercy, pity, pardon, life, having all been rejected, what now is left but wrath, destruction, vengeance, judgment, death? 'The Son of man'—Jesus of Nazareth, the King of the Jews—shall then be on the THRONE, not on the CROSS; and not in Hebrew and Greek and Latin only will this be known, but all men of every tongue shall honour Him as they honour the Father, and shall own as King of kings and Lord of lords this 'Son of man.'

'Marvel not at this: for the HOUR is coming, in the which all that are in the graves shall hear His voice and shall come forth; they that have done good unto the resurrection of life, and they that have done evil unto the resurrection of judgment.' In the first HOUR, which has already lasted more than 1800 years, the dead in tres passes and sins have been getting life; the other HOUR is not yet come, but in it two things will happen. Those that have done good shall be quickened to a resurrection of LIFE—the quickening work of the Son of God being then, and not till then, perfectly completed—He being the 'Omega,' as well as the 'Alpha.' Those that have done evil shall also be raised, but to a resurrection of judgment—which, in their case, shall certainly be eternal damnation. The whole line of thought is judgment (it is the same word as in verses 22 and 24), a judgment not of two Gods but of the one God, who has but one mind and one will, though acting in different persons. All men, saved or lost, shall rise, because Christ is risen.

Reader, in which resurrection will you share—that of life or of judgment? Will you listen to the 'Son of God,' or are you waiting for the judgment of the 'Son of man?' Now is the time of passing from off the ground of judgment through your death, into His life. There will be no change after your spirit has left your body. *Now*, this moment, as you read this line, pause and ask, *Have I passed from death unto life?* If not, hear His voice at this moment; believe His Father's love-message, while you hear 'His word:' 'God so loved the *world*' ('a term co-extensive with its rational and accountable generations') 'that He gave His only begotten Son; that whosoever' (of all the dead, ruined, God-hating sinners in it) 'believeth in Him should' not perish, but have everlasting life.' 'This Man receiveth *sinners*'—'a designation that misses no one individual of the species.' That you are not already in hell, is due only to the tolerance of that God against whom you are daily sinning. This is the HOUR of grace, of life, of pardon: the next HOUR must be the HOUR of vengeance, of judgment, of wrath. Sooner or later you shall know these *realities*. If you get into heaven at all, it must be by hearing His word and believing Him. Then why not now? Are you afraid of making sure of being in heaven too soon? It is heaven on earth, if you but knew it, to be *alive in a living Christ*. Why not antedate your heaven by beginning it now, even if you knew your hour would lengthen out ever so long? All will yet be raised by the power of the living Christ. But what a difference in the doom of the two classes who are raised by Him! One is raised because His Spirit dwells in them; the other, because He is the powerful Judge that condemns them to the lake of fire for ever.

VII. THE BOOK CLOSED AND OPENED.

In Isa. lxi. 1, we read, 'The Spirit of the Lord God is upon me, because the Lord hath anointed me to preach good tidings unto the meek, He hath sent me to bind up the broken-hearted, to proclaim liberty to the captives, and the opening of the prison to the bound; to proclaim THE ACCEPTABLE YEAR OF THE LORD, and the *day of vengeance of our God.'* And in Luke iv. 18, when the Lord Jesus in the synagogue applies this to Himself, He finishes with 'the acceptable year of the Lord.' He does not go on to say, 'the day of vengeance of our God;' but it is written, 'He closed the book, and He gave it again to the minister, and sat down.' What a gospel is in this omission! On it has hung the forebearance of these eighteen centuries. What love, what long-suffering, is in that word, '*He closed the book,*' that book which spoke of vengeance! The proclamation in this hour is, 'the acceptable year of the Lord'—grace, life from the Son of God; but what a day that will be when the book is opened, 'the day of vengeance of our God,' the execution of the judgment of the Son of man

In Rev. v. we see the acceptable year has revolved, the redeemed, worshipping, praising elders are gathered around Himself, and now the book is brought forward, and one of the elders says, 'Behold, the lion of the tribe of Juda, the root of David, hath prevailed to *open the book,* and to loose the seven seals thereof.' This is the book of terrible wrath, the opening of the seals of which inaugurates fearful judgment upon a Christ-rejecting world. Will you be under the vials of wrath, or will you hear of life? 'The book' is closed as yet. He has handed it to His servants; He has left them to proclaim His grace, His gospel, and He has *sat down* waiting till His enemies are made His footstool. What a gospel

A closed book of vengeance, an open heaven, a preached gospel, a seated Christ, life from the Son of God! What a day is coming! An open book of wrath, the door of mercy shut, no more room, a Christ risen up, judgment executed by the Son of man!

Let me, in conclusion, place before you the teaching of Scripture concerning judgment as to a believer. There is,

1st, THE JUDGMENT OF SIN.

This was at Calvary when Christ stood in the place of the sinner, putting away sin by the sacrifice of Himself. He was made sin for us, bare our sins in His own body on the tree, was wounded for our transgressions, was bruised for our iniquities, when God laid our iniquities on Him. This was when He cried, 'My God, My God, why hast Thou forsaken Me?' That was for us. Believing in Him this judgment can never alight on us. If we reject Him, this will be our doom in an eternal hell. It is this judgment spoken of in the passage above quoted from John v., that the believer is beyond. He is no longer a convict. He is a son. He has not to meet the sentence of a judge. He is under authority to Jesus Christ his Lord, and as such he will be judged; but how great the difference! He will not be judged to see whether he is a convict or a servant; he will be judged as a servant.

2d. THE FATHER'S JUDGMENT OF US AS SONS.

We have been now made sons, and are looked upon as being in the Father's home and members of His holy family, and here we find that the judgment or discipline of His house is a present and constant thing, 'If ye call on the Father, who without respect of persons judgeth according to every man's work, pass the time of your sojourning here in fear.' (1 Pet. i. 17.) 'And ye have forgotten the exhortation which speaketh unto you as unto children, My son despise not thou the chastening of the Lord, nor faint when thou art rebuked of Him: for whom the Lord loveth He chasteneth, and scourgeth every son whom He receiveth. If ye endure chastening, God dealeth with you as with sons; for what son is he whom the father chasteneth not? But if ye be without chastisement, whereof all are partakers, then are ye bastards, and not sons. Furthermore we have had fathers of our flesh which corrected us, and we gave them reverence: shall we not much rather be in subjection unto the Father of spirits, and live.' (Heb. xii. 5-9.)

Here also we find the place for practical self-judgment. 'If we would judge ourselves we should not be judged.' If this however is not done, the Lord takes us in hand not for our condemnation but for the very opposite. 'But when we are judged we are chastened of the Lord that we should not be condemned with the world.' (1 Cor. xi. 31, 32.)

Church discipline is also for a similar end, 'In the name of our Lord Jesus Christ, when ye are gathered together and My spirit with the power of our Lord Jesus Christ, to deliver such an one unto Satan for the destruction of the flesh that the spirit may be saved in the day of the Lord Jesus.' (1 Cor. v. 4, 5.)

3d, THE JUDGMENT-SEAT OF CHRIST.

'We must all appear before the judgment-seat of Christ.' This is future and is based on our relationship as servants of our Lord, owning the Lordship of Christ, and responsible to manifest Him now; see, also, Romans xiv. 10, which so clearly shows our individual responsibility to Christ's judgment-seat alone. Every Christian shall render his account of everything he has done.

As a servant the believer shall give account of

1. His works—'Ye shall be recompensed at the resurrection of the just.' (Luke xiv. 14.) 'Behold I come quickly and my reward is with me, to give every man according as his *work* shall be.' (Rev. xxii. 12.)

As to their *quantity*. 'It came to pass that when he was returned having received the kingdom, then he commanded those servants to be called unto him to whom he had given the money that he might know *how much* every man had gained by trading.' (Luke xix. 15.)

As to their *weight*. 'The Lord is a God of knowledge, and by him actions are weighed.' (1 Sam. ii. 3.)

As to their *quality*. 'Now if any man build upon this foundation, gold, silver, precious stones, wood, hay, stubble, every man's work shall be made manifest—for the day shall declare it, because it shall be revealed by fire, and the fire shall try every man's work of *what sort* it is. If any man's work abide which he hath built thereupon he shall receive a reward. If any man's work shall be burned he shall suffer loss; but he himself shall be saved; yet so as by fire.' (1 Cor. iii. 12-15.)

2. His words. 'I say unto you that every idle (unworking) *word* that men shall speak, they shall give account thereof in the day of judgment.' (Matt. xii. 36.) Of course as we have clearly seen this can never be for the damnation of the believer, but should be an incentive to us now; 'Let your speech be always with grace seasoned with salt.' (Col. iv. 6.) 'Be swift to hear, slow to speak.' (James i.—read the whole chapter.)

3. His thoughts. 'Therefore judge nothing before the time until the Lord come, who will make manifest the *counsels* of the hearts; and then shall every man have praise of God.' (1 Cor. iv. 5.) 'The Lord hearkened and heard, and a book of remembrance was written before Him for them that feared the Lord, and that *thought* upon His name. And they shall be mine saith the Lord of hosts in that day when I make up my jewels, and I will spare them as a man spareth his own son that serveth him.' (Matt. iii. 16, 17.)

Lightning Source UK Ltd.
Milton Keynes UK
12 April 2010

152558UK00001B/82/P